The woman's guide to starting your own

In the same series:

Women can return to work
Women can achieve career success

The woman's guide to starting your own business

Where to start and how to make it work

Deborah Fowler

GRAPEVINE

First published 1988

© Deborah Fowler 1988

Cover illustration: Photography, Richard Winslade; co-ordination and styling, Sally Rowat. Scarlet outfit, Laurel; black and white jacket and sweater, Jaeger; jewellery, Imaginca and Butler and Wilson; leather briefcase and planner, Mulberry.

Cartoons by Angela Martin

All rights reserved. No part of this book may be reproduced or utilized in any form or by any means, electronic or mechanical, including photocopying, recording or by any information storage and retrieval system, without permission in writing from the Publisher.

British Library Cataloguing in Publication Data

Fowler, Deborah
   The woman's guide to starting
   your own business: where to start and
   how to make it work.
   1. Small business—Great Britain—
   Management 2. Women-owned business
   enterprises—Great Britain
   I. Title
   658'.022'0941   HD62.7

ISBN 0-7225-1546-4

Grapevine is an imprint of the Thorsons Publishing Group, Wellingborough, Northamptonshire, NN8 2RQ, England

Printed in Great Britain by
Mackays of Chatham, Kent

10 9 8 7 6 5 4 3 2 1

Contents

Introduction 7

1 **Personal circumstances** 9
   Family commitments 9
   Personal financial position 11
   Attitude of mind 15
   Time and motion 18

2 **Qualifications and experience** 21
   Identify your skills 21
   Product knowledge 24
   Commercial experience 26

3 **Training** 27
   Formal training 27
   Retraining 28
   Informal training 29

4 **Choosing your business** 31
   Market research 32
   Index of business ideas 35

5 **Financing your business** 58
   Assessing your financial requirements 58
   Borrowing money – sources of finance 66
   How not to borrow money 71

6 **Taxation and social security** 74
   Income tax 74
   National Insurance 78
   Social security benefits 80

Corporation tax 84
Value added tax 84
Capital gains tax 86
Inheritance tax 87

7 **Business location** 88
   Working from home 88
   Renting a property 94
   Buying a property 98

8 **Business structure** 100
   Sole trading 100
   Partnerships 102
   Limited companies 105
   Buying an existing business 107
   Franchising 108

9 **Selling and marketing** 111
   Selling 111
   Marketing 117
   Advertising 118
   Public relations 120

10 **Day-to-day running** 124
   Book-keeping 124
   Computers 130
   Employing people 133
   Professional advisers 139
   Insurance 141

11 **Success and failure** 146
   Coping with expansion 146
   Recognizing the danger signals 148

Bankruptcy, receivership and
   liquidation 150
Cashing in on success 153

Conclusion 155
Useful addresses 156
Books, leaflets and courses 158
Index 159

Introduction

In recent years, I have written books on almost every aspect of small business life. However this subject, above all others, is particularly close to my heart because it is a very personal one. When my daughter, Lucy, was still a tiny baby, circumstances suddenly dictated the need for me to take over sole responsibility for keeping us both fed and providing us with a roof over our heads. I was determined not to farm Lucy out to a child minder and go back to work in a conventional sense but, still, the bills had to be paid. The result? I started my own small business – with no capital, no permanent home and at a time when the political climate offered very little in the way of practical support for the would-be entrepreneur. Added to this... *I was a woman.*

In today's world, where sexual equality is a recognized requirement of civilized living, you may be tempted to believe that there can be no difference between a man or a woman starting out in business. Frankly, that is rubbish. If you wish to start your own money-making scheme, you need to recognize that you will have to be not only as good as, but actually better, than your average male counterpart. Why? The answer is two-fold. A very real prejudice does still exist towards women in business. More often than not, you will find that people – and to be fair this includes women as well as men – will consider you are just 'playing at it', filling in time before marriage or having a little hobby to keep you occupied while your husband is at work. The other problem is the rod we make for our own backs. Most women enjoy making a home and child-rearing. Whether at one end of the scale, you are simply cooking supper for the man you love or, at the other, demand feeding a new-born baby every three hours, these things are time-consuming, emotionally wearing and tend to take one's eye off the commercial ball. The question that women in business ask themselves far more often than any man will do is, 'Can I justify what I am doing and have I got my priorities right?' It is a never-ending question and attached to it is bound to be an element of guilt. Combining, efficiently, both business and home life does take a fair amount of dedication and hard work.

There are so many reasons why you might have picked up this book. Perhaps, like me all those years ago, you are faced with a crisis. Perhaps time is hanging heavy on your hands because your children have grown up or because you have recently retired. Perhaps you are out of work and see no hope of gaining employment in your particular area or field of experience. Maybe you have recently left school or college and are attracted to the idea of being your own boss rather than settling for conventional employment. Whether your ambitions are to take the business world by storm or merely contribute a few extra pounds to the family's weekly income – opportunities abound.

Never before in this country has there been so much practical help and genuine enthusiasm directed towards private enterprise, but if you are going to start your own business – big or small – then you have got to do it right, and that is what this book is all about. So, let's make a start!

Deborah Fowler

1 Personal circumstances

Family commitments

Picture the scene: it is Monday morning, predictably you are running late and you are due to meet a very important customer. If the meeting goes well, it could solve your income position for the next year – if not, you are going to be in trouble at the bank. You have just finished breakfast when your small son throws up all over the kitchen floor.

What do you do? You bundle him into the car, tell him he is going to feel all right in a minute and take him to school. You promise the teacher you will ring as soon as your meeting is over and you reassure your son that he is already on the mend. Two hours later, you telephone the school and the teacher informs you, in a voice thick with implied criticism, that your son has been sick three more times, he is very distressed and clearly the right place for him is at home. Chances are you made a nonsense of that meeting with the potential customer anyway, because you arrived late, fraught and preoccupied. So, everyone has lost out – your son, your customer and, most of all, yourself. You tried to do two jobs at once and you succeeded in doing them both – badly.

Of course, children stand out as the particular challenge to any woman contemplating running her own business, but you do not have to be a mother to have a conflict of interest. Your partner has an important client he wishes to invite to dinner; you want to attend a trade exhibition that will involve a long journey. What will you do – you will skip the exhibition, if you want a quiet life. One of your parents is ill, the other badly panicking. Is it your brother who will take over the reins and cope? No, more often than not, it will be you – location willing, for women tend to automatically find themselves in the caring role. It is wonderful to be needed but it is a very real commitment of both time and energy.

Recognize all this, therefore. Take a long, cool look at your life and see what personal commitments you have *now* and what you are likely to have in the future. Do you think that, ultimately, your mother or father is going to have to come and live with you? Is your daughter expecting a baby, intending to go back to work and will be looking to you to play the doting grandmother, three days a week? Does your partner have a job that takes him abroad a great deal, and does he like you to travel with him? What are the implications of your not fulfilling these commitments?

Whatever you do, do not fall into the trap of being bolshy. It is no good saying, 'It's my right to have more time to myself. He can walk out of the house in the morning, without a care in the world. Why can't I?' These are not constructive thoughts and, certainly, if you begin to let your commitments slip, without proper planning, far from showing your ungrateful family the error of their ways, it is you who will end up feeling unhappy, angry and guilty.

My advice to any woman who has young children and wishes to start her own business is to try, if humanly possible, to run the business from home. It is fine farming out children for a few hours a week, but it is not fair to have them dumped in other people's homes on a regular basis – they need to be in their own. The alternative, of course, is to employ a full-time mother's help or nanny, but you are talking about a great deal of money and it is a daunting thought to realize that you will have to earn the nanny's salary first before you even begin to show a profit. Many highly successful businesses have started from home and, whether you have children or not, if space will allow, it is an ideal way to begin. In addition, if you are not sure how your family is going to react to this new demand on your time, by starting your business from home, you are not committing yourself too heavily, until you see how everyone adjusts to the new arrangements.

One of the best ways to avoid resentment is to involve the family in your business. It may not be possible if you are a computer programmer, for example, to actually involve either partner or children in physical help. Nonetheless, you can seek their advice on decisions and direction.

Rather than storm out of the room saying you must have more time to yourself, plan your life more carefully. Sit down on a weekly basis and schedule your work times, as far as possible, to convenience everyone. I have worked all my daughter's life and the only time she resented it was when, for a brief period, I was employed by someone else. For the first time, she now tells me, she saw my work as a threat – I was not spending time with her, because I was doing my beastly job. In fact I have always worked far longer hours when running my own business but Lucy could not be involved when I was employed, nor could I organize my work times around her and the resulting tantrums were horrible to behold!

Recognize that the man in your life may well see your business activities as a threat, too, particularly if you are successful and he is going through a bad patch. Be cautious not to rub his nose in your success unless he can match it. Of course, you have every right to be proud of your achievements and he should be pleased for you, but human nature being what it is, pick your moments to bathe in your own reflected glory! Just as with children, time spent on your business is time not spent with him. If you are married and your husband has been used to coming home to the aroma of a gently simmering casserole, he is not going to be enamoured by a telephone call from a Motorway service station 250 or so miles away telling him that you will be home in three hours and could he therefore sort out some supper for himself.

It is all obvious advice, perhaps, but if you do not plan for your family's continued welfare, it is so easy to create bad feeling towards your business that you will never be able to eradicate. Planning is the secret. There will have to be some changes in the family routine and if you are going to start your own business, you need to recognize that you will work harder than you have ever done in any job. You will be preoccupied and distant, tired and frequently bad-tempered – accept this and plan for it, whether it means allowing yourself quarter of an hour in the pub to unwind before going home, eating out once or twice a week, lowering the standards of your housework or sending the washing to the laundry. Look at ways of reducing stress *before it happens*. If you are to succeed at your own money-making scheme, a vital ingredient is your family support and backing. You will not make it *despite your family*, you will make it with their co-operation, or you will not make it at all. Recognize that fact and keep it in the forefront of your mind, at all times.

Personal financial position

Deciding to start your own business is one of the major decisions of your life – at least it should be, if you are taking it as seriously as you should. If your attitude to starting your business is 'Well, I'll have a crack at it and see how it goes' then forget it, because you are not going to succeed. Either take the view that you are going into business to make a success of it, in a wholehearted, committed way or do not attempt it at all.

Your personal financial position, obviously, will play a major part in your decision. Clearly, if you are already severely in debt, the chances of your being able to launch yourself successfully into a new venture are very slim. Alternatively, it could be that the way your present finances are structured, it is simply not worthwhile your earning any more money, because of the tax implications. In this case, perhaps you would be better off doing voluntary work. In between these two extremes there are a myriad of complications relating to tax and National Insurance, where it may be worthwhile your earning £5,000 but not £10,000 or conversely, £10,000 but not £5,000. In Chapter 6, we will explore in detail the implications of tax and National Insurance. Suffice to say here that you need to keep the thought firmly in your mind that additional income obviously will affect your current financial status but not necessarily to any great advantage.

The most sensible way to assess the financial implications of starting a business is to conduct your own personal audit. This means producing a form – along the lines of the example on page 13 that will detail both your present position and your anticipated position in 12 months' time having started your business. You will see I have included a column headed 'Financed By' for you to detail how you are going to cope *personally* in the early months of trading. The object of this personal audit is not to consider how you finance your business – that is a completely separate issue – what I am attempting to ask you to look at, at this stage, is your own personal income and expenditure and how it will be affected. Currently, you may be employed and earning a salary of, say, £6,000 a year. You want to leave your job and start your own business and you feel you can do it because your partner has just been awarded a substantial pay rise. That is all very well, but his pay rise is unlikely to have been £6,000 a year and it will take you some time to put yourself into an income earning position again. Add to that the fact that, if you have a young child, you will have to employ a baby minder, that you will be buying more convenience foods and that your wardrobe is likely to need revamping because you cannot visit your customers in jeans. Suddenly, it becomes obvious that, irrespective of the financing of your trading, your personal income is going to need a vital injection of cash in order for you to contemplate starting your own business. The column 'Financed By' is asking you the direct question – where is this additional money coming from?

One thing you must not do is to use money raised for your business to prop up any personal shortfall. That money is sacred and must be used only for stock, equipment, and so on. Maybe you could take out a second

NAME:			AGE:	
STATUS:	Single	Married	Divorced	Widowed
CHILDREN: Number: Ages:		DEPENDENTS YES/NO		

	PRESENT POSITION (net of tax)	ANTICIPATED POSITION in 12 months' time, net of tax	FINANCED BY (net of tax)
ANNUAL INCOME: Earned by yourself Earned by your partner Private pension plan State pension Child allowance Supplementary benefit Bank interest Building society interest Investment income Total			
ANNUAL EXPENDITURE Mortgage repayments/rent Interest on loans Day-to-day living costs School fees Holidays Entertaining/entertainments Insurance premiums Other commitments Total			
BALANCE surplus/shortfall			
ASSETS House (full value, including mortgage) Additional properties Bank deposits Other deposits Investments Personal possessions Total			
LIABILITIES Mortgages Loans Hire-purchase Credit cards Other borrowing Total			
BALANCE surplus/shortfall			

mortgage on your home or apply for a Gold card. Maybe you have sufficient capital salted away or you feel you can economize (watch this last one, though – as a general rule, you are far more likely to spend more, rather than less, when you go into business, because of the pressure on your time). Long before you consider the financial viability, or otherwise, of your intended business venture, you have got to decide whether you can survive while you are building the business. If you are single, it may appear easier, but it can prove considerably more difficult. On the one hand, you do not have a second income coming into the house to support you, on the other, of course, you do not have the same family commitments. It might be possible, for example, to go home and live with your parents for a few months while you get established or stay with a particularly generous friend who is only going to charge you a peppercorn rent. If you are opting out of safe employment or a regular dole cheque, you have to recognize that something has to give – if you are not earning as much, then you have to spend less.

The other way of looking at the problem is to simply say, 'I cannot go into business unless I am going to earn a minimum of £x.' Then, award yourself a reasonable salary from the start-up of your business and borrow sufficient money to finance it.

Certainly, this can work. My husband went into business with a colleague some years ago. They were starting out in an industry they both knew well and they sat down together to do their financial planning, to establish what sort of capital structure their business would need. When my husband asked his colleague where they should start, the colleague replied, 'Well, I need an annual salary of £30,000 a year, in order to have the kind of lifestyle I want.' So the first figure they wrote down was Managing Director's salary, £30,000! He has drawn his salary cheque from that day to this.

However, with many smaller, less ambitious, businesses, it is usually not possible for the principal to draw anything like the money he or she could earn as an employee – at any rate in the first couple of years. What I am asking you to do is to recognize this and see if your family budget can cope during this start-up period.

Attitude of mind

As already discussed, there are any number of aspects you should consider before you even contemplate taking the first step towards your own business. However, the single most important question that you will ever ask yourself in relation to your business is, 'Have I the right attitude of mind for running a business of my own?'

Forget whether you have any capital, whether the business is a mad scheme, whether you have the necessary skills or even if there is a market out there. All of that we will look at in detail, but first, you have to be sure that you are the right person to run a business – any business. You need to recognize that ultimate responsibility is very lonely and sometimes very frightening. Many of today's top management earning fabulous salaries, when pressed, would admit that they need the security of employment and, ultimately, a boss to make the big decisions. When you are running your own business, the buck stops with you. If things go right, the glory is all yours but if they go wrong, there is no one else to blame but yourself.

A friend of mine said to me, quite recently, that she would like to start her own business and I asked her why. Her reply was that she was fed up with being ordered around by the various bosses she had worked for in her 26 years: 'I want to have my own business, so I can be independent and not answerable to anyone,' she said, with considerable emotion. On the face of it, it sounds all right, doesn't it? She, surely, is a perfect candidate for running a business with her strong, independent nature. I told her to go away and think of a better reason. Look at it like this: if you are employed, your boss is likely to put up with quite a lot from you – you can be late for work now and again and have a period of working badly because you have personal worries, take time off sick and answer back when you feel your boss is expecting too much. Assuming that your quality of work is average, your boss will accept all this. There is no way he or she is going to ask you to leave because there is too much hassle involved. Your boss has trained you, has become used to having you around and there is always the threat of an industrial tribunal if you are sacked. In the average job, you can jog along and get away with murder – not so in your own business.

My friend thought her bosses had been tyrants – that is nothing compared with the average customer. If you have your own business and you interest someone in buying what you have to offer, then you have to be prepared to move heaven and earth to get that sale. The only way to succeed in a small business is to make sure that the customer is King – personal and reliable service is the one thing you have to offer that most large companies cannot achieve. My friend, in swapping her boss for her customer, is only swapping one tyrant for another and, in fact, placing herself at the mercy of an infinitely more powerful and demanding one.

Ask yourself the question – why do you want your own business? Do

you want to be rich and famous, do you want to change the world? Do you want to be more fulfilled in your work, spend more or less time working than you do currently? Before so much as considering *how* you do it, look at what you ultimately want to achieve, for unless you have a goal, you are unlikely to be able to maintain the momentum along the rocky path that is inevitable in the development of any business.

What do you need, in a practical sense, to contemplate running your own business?

- good health
- a steady nerve – without being irresponsible, you have to be able to take risks, albeit calculated ones
- to be a worker – if you are lazy by nature, accept it, but recognize it is not a quality that can qualify you for running your own business
- to be an innovator – in other words, there are a lot of very talented people around, who are good at administering other people's bright ideas, but could not begin to think up any of their own. Being an innovator does not stop with having a bright idea, it is an ongoing process, finding new markets, adapting the product, developing the service and so on
- to have confidence in yourself and your abilities – no shrinking violet ever made it in business. Of course,

we all have our moments of self-doubt, it would be foolish not to. Equally, though, if you are the kind of person who stumbles at the first word of criticism, then you need to recognize that in your own business, you will fall at the first fence.

Let's face it – there are plenty of inventive and interesting things you can do in life besides dashing helter skelter into business. A careful self-analysis may well highlight, in your own mind, the knowledge that the rough-and-tumble of commerce is really not for you. If so, have the maturity to recognize it for, unfortunately, the easiest person in the world to delude is yourself.

Time and motion

There is so much to do. Regardless of the size of your business, the preliminary work alone, never mind the actual running of it, will demand an awful lot of time. In fact, in most respects, the smaller the business the more actual physical work you will have to do. Firstly, you have to organize your product or service into a presentable state so that it can be sold. In the case of a product – particularly if you are planning to manufacture it yourself – there are hours of work involved in finding the right raw materials at the right price, the right equipment and packaging. You have to fine-tune your manufacturing skills to the point where the whole exercise is cost-effective, whilst still good quality and value for money. In theory, providing a service involves less preliminary work, since what you are offering is your skill and your time. Nonetheless, *how* that skill and time is presented will make all the difference to your success or failure.

When you have reached the point where you have something to offer, you then have to find out if it is what the market wants, decide what premises you need, how many staff, how much capital... the list is endless. Successful time and motion in business start-up is largely a question of gearing. If your time is limited, then accept the fact that it may take you two or three years to establish your business, rather than six months, if you were doing it full-time. It is back to personal circumstances. If, for whatever reason, you are not able to give up your existing employment until you have established your business, you will have to look on it as a part-time occupation. What applies to the need to keep earning, could equally apply in the case of family commitments. You might start a business when your youngest child is three, in the hopes that you can build

it into a full-time occupation by the time that child goes to primary school. I cannot stress it enough – most of what goes wrong in the establishment days of a business is all due to lack of planning. Many a potentially good business has failed because the principal has not been able to stay alive in a financial sense long enough to see his or her dreams come true. Everything always takes longer than you anticipate, if for no other reason than that you are so beholden to other people. The customer you anticipated would give you your first major order, may well do so, but they may not require it until the spring when you had anticipated it in the autumn – you have to survive in the meantime.

When people are starting out in business, their primary concern always seems to be about money. Finance is certainly one of the major factors, but to place it in importance above all the others is to work on a false premise. *If your money-making scheme is viable, you will always find the capital to finance it.* What should be taxing you initially is the distribution of your time.

Time is the most valuable commodity you have to offer and it is often – all too often – underestimated. Try and assess realistically, not only how much time you have available but also how much time you need. Then consider how that time could be best spent. Supposing, for example, your Auntie Maud has died and left you £30,000. You find your

job undemanding and it occurs to you that one way you could employ this unexpected capital is to start your own business. Fine, there is nothing wrong with that, it is a good idea. However, ask yourself why is your job so undemanding? Is it because this is what you have set out to achieve for yourself, either consciously or subconsciously. Maybe you have a hectic social life or are obsessed with wind surfing. Perhaps you like going skiing for a month every winter or perhaps you value your family life above everything and your job will always play second fiddle. In these circumstances, you probably would be better advised to use Auntie Maud's £30,000 to, say, buy a holiday cottage that the family could all enjoy and that you could let for part of the year to provide additional income.

You will have the added interest of maintaining the cottage, a growing asset and an extra source of enjoyment for the family. Without doubt, you would have to work very long hours for some years before, shall we say, the manufacture of ceramic mugs would begin to compete in terms of financial gain with your holiday cottage. It is a balancing act and only you can decide the right level of activity for yourself, but to overestimate your available time is courting disaster – not only that, it is placing an intolerable burden upon you. Your moneymaking scheme, whatever it is, has to be enjoyable – if it is not, you will fail at it.

Right, enough heart searching. If you are confident you can cope – let us look at what you can do to achieve your ambitions.

2 Qualifications and experience

Identify your skills

Without doubt, we all perform better when we are doing things we enjoy. Working at something that either does not interest us or that we find somewhat beyond us is very frustrating. It also means, in a competitive sense, we will not produce goods or services of a quality comparable to someone who enjoys what they are doing and has the necessary skills. Take any classroom in the country – the subject that each individual child enjoys will be the one that he or she does best. What applies to children and school work, applies equally well to adults and business.

There are two areas of skill you need to look at. First of all, you need to decide what *sort* of person you are and, secondly, having established that, you need to look at what area of business is most likely to suit you.

We will begin with you. Are you by nature a saleswoman or are you a doer? Are you, perhaps, a creative person who likes producing things, but is intimidated by the prospect of selling? Are you an administrator? Perhaps your forte is the mechanics of business – organizing the records, typing the letters, ensuring that orders go out on time and that customers pay when they should. These different aspects of business life are all needed, to greater or lesser degrees, in every business and, certainly, if you are intending to operate your money-making scheme alone, you need a little of each of these skills.

However, what is important is to

go into a business that will maximize your primary skill. If you are a brilliant saleswoman you might become an agent for your local craft workshops, selling their goods to shops around the country. This would make maximum use of your selling skill but, if you were handling many different types of merchandise from different sources, you would also need a degree of administrative skill as well. As an alternative, if you have always wanted to be, say, a glass blower and love the idea of being on your own in a workshop all day, that is fine – provided you recognize that you need to structure your business so that somebody else will sell your products for you. It could be sensible to take on a partner to do the selling, or maybe you can sell your glass wholesale, but in that case you will have to produce it in sufficient quantities. If you are a good administrator you might decide to set up your own employment agency. Again, this is a fine choice as it would make maximum use of your skill, but somehow you have to attract both clients and would-be staff to use your agency. So, here again, you are going to need to develop a degree of selling expertise as well, or employ someone else who can do that job for you.

Recognizing the type of person you are is the first step towards deciding what field of business life you should enter. Having decided that, you then need to look more specifically at your existing skills in terms of both qualifications and experience. Make a list – this may seem somewhat pedantic but it is surprising what you forget you have actually achieved unless you commit yourself to paper. It is important to put everything down – the Christmas job you took working in a pub ten years ago, the summer you spent looking after children in France – leave out nothing. Then, when your list is complete, let your imagination run riot and consider what, of all those different experiences, you really enjoyed the most. At this point you may well say that you have already decided on your type of business and you thought this book would tell you how to go about it. Fair enough, but, still, go through this exercise. At this point you can be totally flexible. Once you start committing yourself to equipment, finance, staff, premises or whatever else you need, you have lost that flexibility. At the moment, you have the heady sensation of being a free agent and the world is your oyster.

Of course, flights of fancy have to be tempered with realism. You may say that what you've always really wanted to do is to be a portrait painter. The reason you are not already is possibly or even probably because you do not have the talent. On the other hand, what is that Art 'A' level doing under your heading of

qualifications? Perhaps a course at your local art college could develop your skills to the point where you could start earning money as a portrait painter. Nothing is impossible, provided you are really enthusiastic about it.

The reverse of the argument is that to enter into a field about which you know nothing substantially reduces your chances of success. Any bank manager will tell you that the highest failure rate in small businesses is amongst those whose principals have had no previous experience of the business in which they have started trading. Certainly, if you are considering investing a large sum of money in your business venture, then I would strongly recommend that you only enter into a field in which you are thoroughly experienced. So many businesses, from the outside, appear easy – little more than common sense in fact – but in reality they are far more complex than they seem. It is not just the technicalities of running a business that are important either – having the right contacts, knowing where to buy raw materials, understanding the market, knowing what price you should be asking – all these are vital factors. You can learn all this the hard way of course, by trial and error, but that can prove very expensive.

If, having identified the business that appeals to you most, you have no experience, there is nothing to stop you going out and getting the skills you need – in other words learning at someone else's expense. Supposing you want to open a delicatessen. You and your friends believe that you can do much of the cooking for it yourselves and you have identified a cheese wholesaler who will supply you daily. However, the fact remains, you have never run a delicatessen before. The sensible solution is to delay a few months before starting your business and go to work in someone else's shop first. There is so much to learn about shelf-life, mark-ups, the lines that are the most popular, those that never sell, the number of staff you need, window display... Play a low profile, learn everything you can and only then open your own shop.

Here is a golden rule: learn how to run your business from your competitors' mistakes, not your own.

Product knowledge

If your business involves any form of manufacture – from a pot of jam to a sofa bed – you need to be very sure that you have thoroughly researched the legislation that may apply to your particular business. If you are going to become involved in any form of catering, then you need a copy of *Your Guide to Food Hygiene* (HMSO). If you are going to make garments, particularly for children, you need to know the BSI standard requirements for labelling, washing instructions and sizing. If you are going to be manufacturing that sofa bed, you need to know the required safety standards for upholstery fillings.

Proper research is vital *before* you start your business, not once it is established and it has been discovered that you are not conforming as you should. If you are simply knitting handmade sweaters for friends, does it matter about labelling? If you are ambitious and you want your business to grow, yes, it does and, right from the very beginning, you need to cost for doing the job properly.

There is also another aspect – not so noble but equally relevant. You will find that if you label, package and present your product to a proper legal format, your products will look infinitely more professional and are far more likely to sell really well. It is so easy, in the beginning of a business, to assume that you can get away with things because of the size of your market. Indeed you probably can cut corners without falling foul of legislation, but it is a very short-sighted attitude. As with every other aspect of your business life, if you are going to do it at all, *do it properly*.

So, you ask, where do I acquire up-to-date product knowledge? The best place to start is to buy a copy of what would be your trade magazine. In almost any industry you enter, you will find there is an appropriate magazine – many of which are for sale in major newsagents. Alternatively, buy or have sight of, a copy of *The Writers' and Artists' Yearbook* (A. & C. Black), which lists virtually every magazine published and will head you in the right direction. *The Writers' and Artists' Yearbook* is available at most good booksellers.

Your Local Authority is another good source of help and advice. Do not assume that, if you tell them you are going to start a business, they will begin snooping and checking up on you. Frankly they have neither the time, nor the manpower. What they do have, however, is a directive from 'on high' telling them that they must give local businesses every support, and you will find them most helpful.

Her Majesty's Stationery Office will have in stock most of the publications you are likely to need. If you live in a rural area, I would recommend that you contact CoSIRA (Council for Small Industries in Rural Areas). Their head office is at 141 Castle Street, Salisbury, Wiltshire SP1 3TP, though they also have local branches. CoSIRA are very well versed on the 'do's and don'ts' of small businesses and, as well as giving you advice direct, they may be able to put you in touch with someone else who has been over the same hurdles as those you are intending to tackle. If you live outside England, what applies to CoSIRA also applies to the Welsh Development Agency and, in Southern Scotland, the Scottish Development Agency and, further north, the Highlands and Islands Development Board. There is also a Northern Ireland Development Office. Keep asking questions, these people are there to help and you should take advantage of it.

Commercial experience

It is a fact that more women than men have little or no commercial experience. Whether this is because they have gone virtually straight from school to marriage or are more attracted to the professions – such as teaching or nursing – I do not know. Whatever the cause of this is, statistically there are significant numbers of women who have had no direct experience of commerce, at any level. What do I mean by 'commerce' in this context? I mean simply good, old-fashioned trading: you have a product or a service to offer and you hand it over in return for an agreed sum of money. That is commerce. Nothing to it, you may say, 'I am involved in commercial transactions every day of the week, when I go to the supermarket!' True, but you are on the receiving end and it is rather different when you are the person offering the goods.

If you have never been involved in any aspect of business life, then before embarking on a money-making scheme yourself, you should obtain some first-hand experience or you should employ or go into partnership with somebody who has. Of course you can learn the basic methods of trading – how to calculate VAT, how to invoice and so on, but you are loading the dice against you if, until you started in business, all this was a mystery. Maybe you have a friend who has a part-time secretarial job and who would not mind earning a few pounds a week extra or, you never know, might even help you for love in the early days. Maybe the man in your life will give you a hand, though be wary of this as it could cause more trouble than it is worth – teaching the fundamentals of book-keeping can be as disastrous to a relationship as being taught to drive!

Certainly, if you have no commercial experience, you will find your dealings with other people more difficult – bank managers, trained in such things, will instantly recognize your lack of experience; potential suppliers will see you coming and put 10 per cent on the price. Being naive can be a charming characteristic, but not in the big, bad world of business. The moment you feel you are getting out of your depth you are at a disadvantage and so is your business. In the next chapter we will be looking at training in some detail. Suffice to say here therefore, that as with assessing your skills and determining the nature and format of your product, so with commercial experience – if you do not have the necessary knowledge then make sure you go out and get it.

3 Training

If you do not have the necessary skill or expertise to run the business of your choice, then why not consider undertaking some form of training? There are essentially three types of training that may be applicable to you:

- formal training
- retraining
- informal training

Let us look at these in greater detail.

Formal training

Formal training can be subdivided again into two sections – part-time and full-time.

Part-time training

If, during your training period, you need to be in full-time employment or you have family commitments that you cannot off-load, then there are any number of evening classes that you can attend. These, in most respects, are just as good as full-time courses and all you have to do is to make local enquiries to find out when, where and what are run. The alternative is a day-release programme. Here you may run into difficulties in that, if you are trying to obtain an additional skill to start a business, asking a current employer to give you day release may rebound on you if your employer discovers your motives. Certainly, on the face of it, if you are intending to train while in full-time employment, probably an evening class is the best bet. Your local Job Centre and Manpower Services Commission will be able to give you full details and, of course, you can approach colleges direct.

Full-time training

Again, for full details in your area, you should contact your local Job Centre or Manpower Services Commission, who both run very comprehensive courses on all aspects of business – from marketing and sales through to technical skills. There is a quite specific training programme called 'Training for Enterprise', whose aim is to provide advice and information for would-be and existing business owners or managers. In addition there is a YTS Scheme for young people, and a training programme called 'The Job Training Scheme', which is a successor to the TOPS course. All of these, in one way or another, could be relevant to you, and it is well worth asking for details on your chosen subject.

Retraining

Retraining may be necessary for you if, say, you live in an area of high unemployment, if your working life to date has been in an industry that is, for whatever reason, in decline or if you have not worked for some time and feel you are out of touch. By contacting the Job Centre or Manpower Services Commission, you can find out about a training programme called 'The Wider Opportunities Programme'. This deals with the specialist needs of people who have been out of work for a long time, whose skills may have become outdated or for whom English is a second language. This scheme is ideal for women who want to return to work after raising a family. There is also a training programme called 'Access to Information Technology' that is geared, as the title suggests, to bringing you up-to-date with the latest technology in a variety of fields. On the whole this scheme is more geared to people who are already in work and is, therefore, likely to take place in the evenings or at weekends.

When thinking of the requirements for an updating of technology, it is also worth considering, in certain instances, the supplier of your equipment. A very good example of this is a word processor. If you have not used anything but a typewriter before but have decided to start a typing agency and recognize the need for a word processor, there is no need to go on a course, in fact, I would suggest that a computer course could be confusing and irrelevant. As part of the package sold to you by most computer hardware companies these days, you will be offered a training programme – sometimes as an extra, sometimes even included in the price. This is by far the best option, since you will be taught, quite specifically, how to operate a particular programme or series of programmes on a particular piece of hardware. What applies to computers, applies to most ranges of advanced technology. For this reason, if you are buying equipment that you feel may involve you in a fairly hefty programme of training, do choose, as far as possible, a local supplier. Having your troubles sorted out long distance is fraught with problems all round.

Retraining is, of course, potentially very frustrating. If you have learned a skill in a particular industry, presumably that skill was your first choice of occupation. The need to retrain in many instances, may be brought about, not because you have personally chosen to change the area of your expertise, but because you have had the decision forced upon you. The thing to remember is that life is all about change and changes are stimulating. The learning of a new skill,

particularly if it is to be applied to the starting of an enterprise of your own, will open up new areas of knowledge and experience for you that, in the long term, may prove far more enjoyable than anything you have done before. Recognize that a retraining programme is likely to take place when you are not particularly young and so picking up the ability of learning again, after perhaps years away from school or college, is not easy. It will take you longer to absorb facts than hitherto and you may find the experience, intially at any rate, rather depressing and bad for your ego. Hang in there – if it is a subject that truly interests you, you will soon become absorbed and, as each week passes, you will find it easier to absorb new facts. Whatever you do, *don't look back.*

Informal training

If you are starting your own business, in many industries, a formalized training programme is neither necessary nor desirable – it is practical experience you need. In the previous chapter we cited the example of a delicatessen, which falls into this category, as, indeed, do most retail trades, many areas of sales and marketing and various service industries. Other areas that you feel need formal training might require quite the reverse. Supposing you are involved in some sort of craft industry, whether it is needlework or pottery or some form of art, you may feel a course could improve your skills and, indeed, you may be right. On the other hand, assuming that you are developing what has been a hobby for some years into a business, a formalized training programme in ceramics, might actually have the effect of squashing the freshness of your individual designs. The kind of experience you need, in these circumstances, is more likely to be in gaining an understanding of your market. Let us continue to use ceramics as an example. You might be turning out beautiful ceramic mugs that you have been giving to friends and family for years and over which they have been consistently raving. No evening class could teach you to make them any better but, after a careful survey of your local retail outlets, you may find that mugs quite as good as yours are selling like hot cakes at half the price, having been imported. This means that if you want to concentrate your selling effort in a localized area, you may have to consider adapting your ceramic skills into making something completely different, which in turn could lead you to a formal training programme, though not necessarily. In other words, what I am saying is this – if you have a talent for producing a particular item, you may not need to develop a greater skill, via a training programme. Informal training, acquired by working in a craft shop for a few months, could give you a far better understanding of what the public are actually looking for and at what price and in what colour, and thus enable you to adapt your work to meet the needs of the market.

Never be afraid to emulate what someone else is doing successfully. You do not have to be a pioneer – in fact pioneers very rarely get rich. Far better to obtain a thorough understanding of a highly successful business and emulate it, though at the same time trying to improve upon it, in colour, range, price, quality, service – whatever you think is the most appropriate.

In very many new business ventures you can obtain all the training you ever need by simply keeping your eyes open and seeing what everyone else is doing and how successful they are at doing it. Consider your own needs and the needs of your friends. What are you all lacking in your particular area? Where does such and such a product or service fall down? Informal training is vital – it is all about understanding your market and that is what we are going to deal with in greater detail in the next chapter.

4 Choosing your business

Market research

One of the most fundamental mistakes that people make when starting a business is to fail to thoroughly research their market – and, in some instances, they actually ignore it altogether. This is particularly true of the cottage industry, dealing, in most instances, in craft goods, which is a type of business that does prove particularly attractive to women. The reason market research is not properly undertaken in these circumstances is because people do not take sufficient account of the fact that there is a vast difference between giving an item away and selling it.

Let us suppose you are a dab hand at pressed-flower pictures or lampshades or crocheted shawls. Initially you develop the skill to satisfy a requirement of your own. Then you make a sample for your mother or your sister or your best friend. Someone on the local Red Cross Committee or Playgroup Fund-raising Committee, learns that you are making these attractive items and asks you to make half a dozen to sell on their stall. They sell within a few minutes and somebody says to you, 'You ought to start a proper business making these things.' At this point it is very easy to become over-excited and manufacture a large stock that will never sell and will lead you into a great deal of fruitless expense. Recognize that anyone who is fond of you enjoys receiving something from you that has been handmade. Recognize that everyone exclaims warmly over a present. Recognize also that even if you have sold one or two items for a profit, you may have already saturated the market in your area. This is really the crux of what you have to establish – how many people, over what length of time, are likely to want what you have to offer and are they going to be prepared to pay enough for it for you to make money out of the venture?

It is vital that you identify your precise market. Think big initially. Look at the whole country, comprised of approximately fifty million people and now start striking off those people who would not be interested in your product or service – it could be men or women or children, old people or young people. Look at the cross-section of society – do your goods appeal to a particular social grouping, urban or rural... break it down again. Is your business regionalized? In other words, are you selling by mail order or to a wholesaler or are you expecting to sell direct to the local community? If, for example, you are running a corner shop in an urban area, you are probably only looking at a few hundred square yards as being the ultimate in market potential.

Having established the size of your market, as you see it, consider the long-term appeal of your product or service. Are you dealing in a fad, a current craze that will be out of fashion in a few weeks, months or years? If so, be very wary. There is nothing wrong in jumping on a fashion bandwagon, so long as you recognize that, at some time in the future, you are going to have to jump off – sooner rather than later – and at that point you have to be able to shed your commitments.

Look, too, at the accessibility of your customers. You might be able to demonstrate satisfactorily to yourself that five thousand people in the country would love to own and could afford to buy, the beautiful reproduction grandfather clocks you are making – but how do you get to them?

Very often, if you are dealing with a specialist product, there is a specialist trade magazine from which you can advertise your wares. For example, if you are making flies for fishermen, there are plenty of fishing magazines. Back to the grandfather clocks though – how do you identify the person with the right taste and sufficient money to be bowled over by your product? In this instance you have to not only establish that there is a market, you have to work out how to reach it.

As part of your market research, you need to study presentation. It is all very well having an attractive product or service, but it must be presented to your would-be customer in the correct way or it will not succeed. You need just the right image. One of the most important aspects to consider is how your product or service compares with the competition in terms of quality, price, presentation and delivery. Put yourself in the position of the customer. Would you favour your product over the competitors? If not, then you have to find a way of making sure you have the edge over the competition.

Recognize that the buyer and the customer may be two different people or, indeed, in some instances, that three different people's tastes can be involved. Supposing, for example, you are in toy manufacturing. You may have produced a toy that your child and his contemporaries adore, but now we have to consider the mother. Mother is the one who is going to have to pay for this much-prized toy, so what you have to think about is whether the toy can be competitively priced so that mother can afford to buy the toy for her child. That, however, is not where the story ends. If you are going to sell this toy on anything like a grand scale, then you are going to have to sell through retail outlets, in which case your true buyer is not the child, nor the mother, but the *buyer of the shop*. He or she will naturally be concerned with price and with child appeal, but has other considerations as well: does the toy look good on a shelf, is it very bulky so it takes up too much space, is it fragile so that breakages are high, does it meet safety standards? In looking at your market, consider the buyer's needs very carefully. Certainly, appealing to the buyer is not the only criteria for if your product does not sell off the shelves, he or she will not buy further stocks from you, but, even so, the buyer's wishes are at least as important as those of your ultimate consumer.

A case history *Some years ago, when my daughter was small, a friend of ours came to see us, to ask me for advice. She had produced an enormous polystyrene ball and had made a series of different covers for it, showing faces of pirates, clowns and teddy bears and a special woolly version for very small children. The ball had been passed by British Standards so far as safety was concerned and it was specially weighted so that it could be pushed along by a baby, in the early stages of walking without rolling too fast causing the child to fall flat on its face. It was brilliant. My daughter was already walking at the time, but she instantly fell in love with it, leap-frogging over it, doing headstands and as a result, we were given a sample!*

At 12, Lucy is still playing with it. She practices her gymnastics on it and I have to say it is the most successful toy she has ever had. However my friend's business did not get off the ground. Why? Because each of these balls she had to sell for £22.50 in order to make any money at all and, even then, she was cutting her profit margin too tight for comfort. Baby Boots were interested, Mothercare were interested, but neither took up selling the ball because they recognized that they would have to sell it for over £50. They assumed, rightly, that £50 was just too much for parents to spend on what, on the face of it, seemed such a simple toy.

In hindsight, I have to say that if I had known the hours of pleasure that ball would give, I would have been more than prepared to pay £50, particularly when one considers the 'five-minute wonders' we buy for our children that are so quickly discarded and never played with again, but only in hindsight. My friend produced a brilliant product, but commercially it never saw the light of day because its merits could not be displayed and so it was not perceived to be good value for money.

Market research is often considered to be something one should do at the inception of a business but I think it is important to stress here that market research should be part and parcel of your ongoing business strategy. In today's changing world, you can never say, 'This is my market and that's an end to it'. Markets change, people change and it is very easy for you to plod on regardless, not noticing these changes and then suddenly find that sales have dropped dramatically. Every few months, particularly if you are in a volatile business, you should take time off to really see what the competition is doing and try to reassess what your customer requires. The success of today is the failure of tomorrow – unless you are prepared to move with the times.

Index of business ideas

As a guide to your selection of the right money-making scheme for you, I thought it would be helpful if I listed some of the opportunities that are available to you, together with brief details. Obviously I have slanted my thinking towards businesses most appropriate to women, particularly if you are working from home, although many of the suggestions could well be built up into large commercial concerns.

The object of this section is to stimulate ideas and for you to consider as wide a span of opportunities as possible. Do look at each section, even if you think it does not apply to you as there may be something that triggers off an idea.

What about one of the traditional craft industries?

Antique furniture restoral

A degree of skill and a natural feel for working with wood is necessary here. A course at technical college can provide you with the skills, then you can either operate the business as a service or buy, restore and re-sell furniture, according to the amount of space and capital you have available.

Artificial flowers

There has been a big resurgence in the popularity of artificial flowers. You can work in anything from paper to exotic silks and satins. Largely a self-taught skill, if your product is good enough, there should be quite a market in local stores.

Bookbinding

There is always a market for bookbinding and book restoring but it is skilled work. There are courses available, and some specialist tools are required, though these are not as expensive as you might think. If you cannot find a course in your area, try apprenticing yourself to an existing bookbinder.

Candle making

You need a fair amount of room to hang the candles while the wax solidifies. Remember, too, that candle making is a high fire risk, so check your insurance. A good book to help you develop the art is *The Simple Methods of Candle Manufacture* (Intermediate Technology Publications).

China repairs

This is skilled work, but there are courses available. You need a steady hand, excellent eyesight and endless patience. A course will teach you the basics but you do need a natural feel. You can offer this as a service or you can buy chipped and broken china and repair it for re-sale.

Egg decorating

The more exotic the egg you have to work with, the higher the price you can command. If you have a natural gift for art, practice on a blown hen's egg and then develop to the more exotic. Eggs are also popular in pottery, wood, china and glass and will sell much better on an egg stand.

Enamelling

Your local technical college will almost certainly run an enamelling course. You need some space, a kiln, tools, glazes and a copper. Here again, enamelling is a fire hazard so do check your insurance. All good craft shops will supply you with raw materials, together with books on the subject.

Glass engraving

This is a craft that is always popular. You can engrave glass with sketches or patterns but perhaps the most popular use for engraving is personalized glass. The Guild of Glass Engravers, 19 Portland Place, London W1N 4BH, will give you details of colleges running glass engraving courses.

Jewellery making

The secret to successful jewellery making is to be able to produce something that is both individual and quite definitely has a recognizable style. Again, there are usually a number of courses run locally and what sort of material you choose to work with depends, not only on your inclination, but on the size of your bank balance. The jewellers' trade magazine is called JEMS and if you have trouble locating a copy, write to their address: 7 Hillingden Avenue, Sevenoaks, Kent TN1 3RB.

Lampshades

Virtually all technical colleges offer lampshade making courses and, because these are very popular, the market for lampshades is somewhat questionable. Offering to make lampshades as a service is unlikely to be very lucrative unless you can track down an interior decorator who will give you regular work. You could make lampshades to sell to your local lighting shop but they will have to be very special and individual to compete with mass-produced shades. There is possibly a market for fun, children's lampshades but do check out safety standards.

Leatherwork

Handbags, wallets, belts, purses – leatherwork is taught at most technical colleges. The tools are not expensive and there is always a market for interesting leatherwork. Aim for quality, though – you cannot compete with imported goods on price so your work is going to have to be very special to warrant its higher price.

Model making

If you have any architectural experience you will find a ready market for your work from architects and planning authorities, who often require scale models. Similarly, some businesses, such as building societies, do from time to time require models to use as display items. On the whole, though, this is specialized work and you do need contacts in the trade.

Painting

You can paint portraits of people or animals, you can be a book illustrator, a cartoonist, design Christmas and birthday cards or, perhaps, specialize in landscape painting of a particular area and sell to tourists. You need talent and a certain amount of luck but, above all, you need to be pushy to get your work sold. If you want to be commercially successful you cannot allow yourself the indulgence of an easily bruised ego. There are plenty of painting courses available at art colleges and technical colleges. This is a delightful hobby that could well earn you money, if you have the right combination of talent and determination.

Photography

Photography can be a money-spinner, but it is not an easy market. You can concentrate on functional photography, working perhaps for your local newspaper or a magazine. Alternatively, you can look on photography as an art form and produce photographs that can be framed and sold. Neither markets are particularly easy to break into. What you need first is a portfolio to demonstrate the range of your work. Again, try and specialize and build a reputation in a specific area. There are plenty of photography courses available.

Picture framing

There are courses on picture framing but setting yourself up in this business is expensive and there is a great deal of competition from the high street. I would suggest that picture framing is not something you should enter into as a money-making scheme in itself. However, if you are intending to earn your living as an artist or a photographer, this could be a useful skill to learn, in order to reduce your overheads and increase your profit potential.

Printing and publishing

The actual mechanics of printing are enormously satisfactory. You can learn to do this at technical college and the costs of a hand-printing machine can be as little as £200 – your college will be able to help you find one. There is quite a market for limited editions of famous works, particularly if they are nicely illustrated. The copyright rule is such that you can publish any book that was first published more than 50 years ago. Apart from book publishing, you could consider offering printing services to local businesses, schools and so on.

Pottery

Undoubtedly one of the most popular crafts. There are plenty of courses available to you. You need a kiln, a potter's wheel, some other basic items of equipment and materials. Again, consider the fire hazard and check your insurance. As with most craft industries, the secret of success with pottery is to produce something individual that is instantly recognizable as your style.

Toy making

The word here is caution, for safety is of paramount importance. Toys have to conform to the Toys (Safety) Regulations 1974 (see leaflet No. SI 1367, available from HMSO). Do study these very carefully before attempting to sell anything you have produced. Once you are satisfied on the safety angle, toys can be quite a lucrative market, particularly at craft fairs. Do not make them too complicated – children like simple things best.

Upholstery, curtains or loose covers

Making curtains you can undertake, perhaps, without any training, but where upholstery and loose covers are concerned, you must be properly trained. There is a City and Guild's Certificate in upholstery that you can obtain and there are a number of courses run by technical colleges. For loose covers and upholstery, you need to be fairly fit for there is a considerable amount of lifting involved. Ideally, if you are offering a service, it is better to include transport – in which case you need a van. You also need a fairly sophisticated heavy-duty sewing machine. Not to be seriously undertaken as a money-making scheme until you are well qualified in the art.

Weaving

Weaving is a wonderfully soothing pastime. Lovely shawls and rugs can be produced by the subtle use of colours and differently textured wools. However, as a commercial enterprise, it is very difficult to see how you can make money, for the process takes so long. Perhaps you could look at the market for woven pictures, for which you might be able to command a high enough price. Most art colleges run weaving courses.

Woodwork and carpentry

If working with wood fascinates you, there are plenty of courses you can attend. You can direct your skills towards wood carving by producing ornaments and small items for the home. Alternatively, you can concentrate on joinery and carpentry and therefore offer your skill as a service. Either way you need to be taught about wood so do attend a course before you start.

How about catering?

A catering business can take many different forms and, if you enjoy cooking and have a natural flair, it is tempting to believe that you can start a business in this area. First though, remember that there is a world of difference between a good cook and a good chef. If you are producing food for the public commercially, it is a very different thing to serving up a sumptuous dish for your family or friends. Costings, speed, hygiene and presentation must all be perfected and, if possible, I would recommend that before you embark on commercial catering you enrol on some form of course from the many that are available. Alternatively, you could apprentice yourself to a professional chef who will teach you more tricks of the trade than you would have believed possible.

Once you feel you have fortified yourself with sufficient skill and knowledge, the first thing you must do is to subscribe to *The Grocer* magazine (5–7 Southwark Street, London SE1 1RQ, telephone 01-407 6981). *The Grocer,* among other things, publishes a list of all the cash and carrys throughout the country and contains a great deal of information that you will find invaluable. Unless you are embarking on catering in a big way initially, do be wary of cash and carrys, for you can find yourself buying in such bulk that you have to throw away vast quantities of food. The other thing to be careful of is prices – many supermarkets can compete with cash and carry prices.

Finally, whatever form of catering you are considering, recognize that the hours are invariably antisocial. If you are running a restaurant or câfé this is obvious, but even if you are doing outside catering for a wedding, then bang goes your Saturday and if you are catering for dinner parties, bang go your evenings.

Well, I have done my best to put you off – now let us look at the various avenues that are open to you!

Cake decorating

There is a considerable market for exotic cakes, particularly party cakes made to specific order for a special occasion. You cannot bake a cake, ice it, sell it to a shop in the ordinary way and compete with the average baker. However, by dealing direct with the general public you can work up a reputation for making very special cakes for very special occasions. You need to be painstaking in your research so that you know the recipient's hobbies and special interests and the finished article needs to look very professional. Achieve this and you can charge well over the odds. Some evening classes provide a cake decorating course or you can enrol at a catering college. You will need an icing turntable but otherwise there are few initial costs involved. Try making cakes for friends and build up a reputation by word of mouth.

Frozen meals

There is a market for frozen meals but the problem is that Marks & Spencer and one or two of the other better quality supermarkets recognize this and are producing some really lovely meals that just need heating. Nonetheless, there is no reason why you should not gain a share of this market, provided you keep your range small, use the best possible ingredients and allow generous helpings (supermarket helpings are nearly always too small). You could aim at individuals or at pubs and small restaurants, who would probably jump at the chance of having one or two ready-made dishes that can be microwaved to order. Work out a menu and have it printed, leaving prices blank so that they can be altered from time to time. Try and acquire second-hand commercial freezers and do not overlook the cost of keeping these going all the year round.

Function catering

You can cater in bulk for weddings or office Christmas parties, you can cater for private dinner parties or business lunches or you can simply provide canapés for cocktail parties – all come under the heading 'function catering' and you could, in fact, offer all of these services. To set yourself up properly, you do need to make a considerable investment in equipment – cutlery, plates, glasses and so on. You also need plenty of room at home – not only to store the equipment but to prepare and store food in advance of a function. For outside catering you will probably require a partner or have to employ someone to help you with the larger functions. You need to have smart business cards printed and flash these around and here again you are more likely to achieve results through word of mouth rather than via an expensive advertising campaign.

Preserves

People love homemade preserves like pickles, chutneys, marmalade and mincemeat and, whilst these items are often available in the country, they are certainly not abundant in urban areas. Presentation is everything – unusual shaped jars with mob caps in attractive fabric will go a long way towards helping you sell your preserves. You can sell direct to the public or to delicatessens. If the product is good enough, why not approach one or two major stores? Make sure you have a properly printed label which, in any case, is required by law. Your label should state your name and address, give description of the contents and the exact weight of the contents. It should also mention the date of production.

Sandwich making

This is a relatively new type of catering that does seem to be catching on fast. If you live in an area where there is a considerable amount of industry, you might consider supplying lunch-time sandwiches. The size of businesses in your area is important – very large companies will have their own canteen, so it is small- to medium-sized businesses that should provide your main customers. Work out a menu of ready-made sandwiches, supply extras like crisps, drinks, biscuits and cakes, and try it out locally. Ideally you should be able to deliver sandwiches daily, against specific orders, though you should always carry an extra stock of sandwiches for unscheduled sales. On the day you deliver, you can collect orders for the following day. There is a firm operating in Holborn, London, who have acquired an off-licence. When I was visiting a publisher not long ago, a girl arrived with my editor's lunch, which consisted of three rounds of beautifully presented smoked salmon sandwiches and half a bottle of Muscadet, chilled to perfection. She even provided a napkin and a very acceptable plastic glass! Of course all this was not cheap, but as my editor pointed out, it was a lot cheaper than eating in a restaurant and quite as delightful. Do be careful about the requirements of the Environmental Health Officer in terms of transport. Ideally, you need a car or van that you use only to deliver sandwiches – obviously, the family car, covered in dog hairs, will not do!

Snack bars, cafés, restaurants

The ultimate in catering, of course, is your own establishment where you invite the public to come and sample your cuisine. What sort of food, décor, price and atmosphere you offer should not be the result of personal preference but a true understanding of your immediate environment and its needs. Although you might dream of an haute cuisine restaurant, serving every imaginable exotic dish, your area may, in fact, need a jolly good café supplying eggs and chips for 12 hours each day. The golden rule here is that, whatever you do, do well and try and make what you are offering just that touch individual and memorable – whether it be in a tiny café or a top restaurant. Keep your menu relatively small and change it from time to time to satisfy regular customers. Keep some stalwart standard dishes for catholic tastes.

The ramifications of obtaining a licence and indeed securing planning permission to operate a restaurant at all are somewhat complicated. You definitely need a solicitor, preferably a solicitor who specializes in dealing with the licenced victuallers trade. Recognize that running this sort of enterprise is very time consuming and that you simply must enjoy living and breathing the business 24 hours a day to even contemplate tackling it.

I perhaps do not seem particularly enthusiastic about the catering trade. I do, in fact, have personal experience, having run a restaurant myself and I have to say it was the hardest three years of my life, and this obviously influences my attitude. What worries me is that a woman with a talent for cooking may be tempted to look on catering as an easy way into commercial life, which it certainly is not. Quite rightly, the laws of the land are fairly tough when it comes to the supply of food and you have to be very thorough in your hygiene standards. In Chapter 7, I deal with this aspect in detail, and there are plenty of helpful leaflets on the subject.

If, despite my warnings you are keen on a business in catering, then good luck, but do play it by the rules.

You could make money as . . .

An actor

You can take up acting at any stage in your life – you do not have to be young. It is an overcrowded profession but if you are prepared to undertake anything, opportunities do present themselves from time to time. You could go to drama college or you could try and persuade a repertory company to take you on as an assistant stage manager, which basically means making the tea! There is also broadcasting to consider and, really, it is never too late to start if you feel you have the talent. Equity, the actors' union, at 8 Harley Street, London W1, will be pleased to offer advice.

An animal minder

There is an increasing market for looking after other people's animals. More people these days have holidays abroad and more families have both partners working but, despite everybody's mobile lifestyle, more people have pets than ever before. You can feed cats and walk dogs without needing to provide kennelling. Certainly, if you are interested in opening a boarding kennel, do first consider your neighbours. If the animals you take into your home make too much noise, your neighbours could put you out of business. You must be sure you are in a position to offer animals adequate space, that is both warm and comfortable, and this tends to come expensive. Ideally, if you can provide services for animals in their own home, it is preferable, at any rate initially.

A beauty therapist

You need training to be a beauty therapist and should write to the National Federation of Beauty Therapists, PO Box 36, Arundel, West Sussex BN18 0SW, which will be able to advise you on the type and scope of courses available. Once qualified, you can either set up your own salon or you can visit people in their own homes, depending really on your circumstances.

A disc jockey

You must be a night owl, you must like people and have an extremely outgoing personality. You also need to have sufficient capital to acquire the necessary equipment – an amplifier, speakers, a microphone, mixers and, preferably, a light show. It is difficult to make a full-time career out of being a disc jockey, although if you are good enough, you will be much in demand, particularly at certain times of the year. You need to advertise your services – looking not just to individuals but to firms, clubs, pubs, schools and colleges to provide you with work. Before going into business you need to obtain a licence from Phonographic Performers Ltd, Ganton House, 14–22 Ganton Street, London W1.

A driver

You can be a freelance driver in a variety of ways – as a taxi driver, as a courier or by simply transporting goods from A to B. You need to genuinely love driving, you need the right vehicle and, once you are using your vehicle for commercial purposes, you must look both at your licence and insurance position, which will almost certainly need adjustment.

An editor

Editing, proof-reading, manuscript reading, indexing and typesetting, are all freelance skills that the publishing industry require on a regular basis. To find out more information, obtain a copy of *Careers in Journalism* from the National Union of Journalists, 314 Gray's Inn Road, London WC1X 8DP and *The Writers' and Artists' Yearbook* (A. & C. Black) is very useful too. It is vital to have some contacts and experience in publishing and if you are persistent you may well find regular work. Good, fast, reliable service is everything in this business.

A journalist

As with editing, it is helpful to have copies of *Careers in Journalism* (NUJ) and *The Writers' and Artists' Yearbook* (A. & C. Black). There are openings for freelance journalists in both regional and national newspapers. Again, it helps if you know someone who can give you an introduction but, if not, just persevere, producing articles on subjects that interest you and that you feel will be of interest to the public. Plenty will be rejected but eventually one will be accepted and you will be on your way. Be persistent and ask editors why your work is rejected.

A model

Models, like actors, come in all shapes and sizes. *The Creative Handbook*, available from 100 St Martin's Lane, London WC2N 4AZ, lists most model agencies. Get yourself professionally photographed and send copies with a full list of vital statistics to a variety of agencies. Remember agencies are looking for all types of models – not just the standard 'glamour puss'. From time to time, they require the housewife type, the spinster type, the granny and the lady tycoon. If you do not have a model figure, you might still find you can get work as a character model.

A musician

However talented you may be as a musician and regardless of your musical preferences, you need to recognize that in order to make money you have to also learn to be a performer. There are precious few openings in the music business. Usually you will have to create your own by establishing a jazz band, a choral ensemble or whatever and then slowly build a reputation. Alternatively, you could teach music, which might not be so exotic but will certainly provide you with a more regular income.

An odd job woman

Every community needs its one or two treasured odd job men, so why not an odd job woman? You need to be skilled in plumbing, understand electrics, be able to fix shelves and undertake painting and decorating jobs. All of these skills can be learned at technical college and there is no reason why such services should not be undertaken by a woman rather than a man. In fact, in today's violent world, undoubtedly you will have the edge over a man as other women will often feel far more comfortable about letting you rather than a man into their home. This is an area where far more women should become involved.

There are never enough of these skills to go round and if you are efficient and turn up when you say you will, you cannot fail to run a highly successful business. Think of your experiences of workmen who never appear or who leave a terrible mess for you to clear up – it would not be very difficult to be better than them, would it?

A writer

I could wax lyrical for pages and pages about the joys and sorrows of being a writer because that is *my* job! The most important thing about writing is not to expect to be an overnight success. Unknowns do write best-sellers and become millionaires, seemingly overnight, but for every one of them, there are thousands of people like me, who earn a good, steady income by writing from nine to five, five days a week, for fifty weeks of the year. I, personally, do not approve of writing and journalism courses. If you have something to say, then get on with it and commit it to paper. What is far more vital than a course in how to write is to understand and recognize your market, whether you are planning to write a short story, a romantic novel, a work of non-fiction, or whatever. Study the other publications in your field and learn from them. If you are intending to write a book, try and find an agent (*The Writers' and Artists' Year Book* gives you a list of agents). On the whole, if you are intending to write a full-length book, it is better to try and sell it on the basis of a synopsis and a couple of sample chapters. This saves a potential agent having to plough through a completed manuscript and ensures that you do not waste too much time on what could be an unsaleable book.

Everyone needs clothes, so how about . . .

Opening a boutique

It is a popular misconception that running a shop is easy. What *is* easy about running a shop is getting into appalling debt very quickly. There are so many pitfalls – the most common of which is ending up with a lot of stock you simply cannot sell. Before opening a boutique, it is wise to work in some form of clothing retail store and look carefully at your local community to make sure that any shop you open really will have a big enough catchment area to support it. Then go slowly, making as little in terms of stock commitment as you can.

Clothes hire

Providing clothes for special occasions is often a viable type of business – look at Moss Bros! There are weddings, of course, and balls and a lot of women need to wear hats once or twice a year but resent buying them. There is also a big market for fancy dress. All you need to do is to allocate a room in your house that is warm and well lit and have one or two flattering long mirrors. Then it is a question of building up stock. You can buy second-hand clothes or you can make your own and, once people know you are in business, you will be surprised how many people will donate items to you. It is then up to you to market yourself and make sure that as many people as possible in your area know of the service you offer.

Crochet

You can either offer your crocheting services to a knitwear manufacturer or designer or you can make and sell your garments direct to individuals or boutiques. Which of these avenues you choose will depend to some extent on where you live. If you are located, for example, close to Nottingham, there are plenty of manufacturers around looking for such services – not so in Oxford, Reading or Torquay. Certainly making and selling garments directly will make you more money, although it will be up to you to market what you make. You will find *The Drapers' Record* (Knightway House, 20 Soho

Square, London W1V 6OT) a helpful source of information for where to buy your raw materials. Try and follow fashion trends – crocheted baby garments are not at all popular these days but crochet as high fashion is. Spend the day in London, going round some of the top stores and buy some of the top fashion magazines for ideas.

Dressmaking

As with crochet, you can either sell your services to a manufacturer or make clothes and sell them direct to the public. You could provide a specialist service for a specific area of the market, such as maternity wear, clothes for large ladies, wedding dresses or whatever. You could build quite a substantial business by offering your particular range of garments for sale by mail order. Alternatively, you could specialize in one particular line and try selling it to a number of shops. Whatever you do, make sure you are very professional in your presentation. All garments should have labels, stating size, country of origin and washing instructions. You need to think up a snappy name for your business to ensure that all your garments are credited to you. Again, head for something really individual and if you find a gap in the market, stick to it. *The Drapers' Record* will be very helpful to you.

Knitting

As with crochet and dressmaking, you are faced with the choice of either offering your services to a manufacturer or working for yourself. With knitting there is the additional choice of whether you are going to knit by machine or by hand. As a general rule these days, I do not recommend machine knitting as a means of earning a living. The machines are not cheap and machine-made garments can be produced so quickly and efficiently by major manufacturers, both at home and abroad, that it is impossible to compete. However, there has been an enormous resurgence of interest in hand-knitted garments, particularly those in bright colours with exotic patterns. If you are a demon knitter, perhaps could get together a team of women around you of similar inclination, then a really snappy pattern could have people screaming for your sweaters. *The British Hand-knitting Association*, PO Box CR4, Leeds LS7 4NA, will supply you with names and addresses of yarn manufacturers. You will also find *The Drapers' Record* very helpful.

Second-hand clothes

Second-hand clothes shops are springing up everywhere. Now that fashion has become such an open-ended affair, what may be out of fashion for one woman is in fashion for another. Where second-hand shops really come into their own, of course, is with children who virtually all grow out of their clothes long before they have worn them out. The best way to operate a second-hand clothes shop, if you can afford it, is to buy in stock, literally paying cash to people who bring you their unwanted clothes. This way they will accept a far lower price than they would do if you simply agreed to display the merchandise and pay them when you made a sale. In addition, of course, it cuts out a lot of administration and if you can actually pay cash in the shop for the stock you purchase, chances are you will have that cash back again ten minutes later when it is spent on some of your existing stock! If you cannot afford to do this then you will have to take in goods on a sale or return basis, in which case you need very careful record keeping to ensure that the right people end up with the right money. You do not need high street premises for this sort of operation – more often than not you will find several women club together to bring a car load so the outskirts of a town is good enough. What you do need is an iron will, to ensure that you do not buy stock you cannot shift.

Can you be of service...

Running an agency

You can run an employment agency, an office cleaning agency, theatre tickets/travel agency, modelling agency, au pair agency – in other words there are a number of different ways in which you can be in business getting for the client whatever goods or services he or she may require, that is, acting as the go-between. You can run an agency from home but you do need to be careful that there are not too many callers at your door or you will start having problems with the neighbours. In theory, all you need is a telephone, a typewriter and a load of contacts in the field of your choice. If your agency involves employing people, for instance, sending out office cleaners, secretaries or whatever, you need a licence from the Department of Employment (for their address, see page 157). To be a successful agent you do need an understanding of the particular business of your choice and you must be very sure that there really is a need for what you have to offer in your area.

Book-keeping

With the upsurge in small businesses, there is an increasing demand for freelance book-keepers. Certainly many entrepreneurs operating alone do not have the time to handle their accounts and sort out their VAT. Provided you have somewhere quiet to work, a desk and a filing cabinet and you are up-to-date with tax legislation, then this is a service you may well be able to offer. The best way to become established is to persuade local bank managers, accountants and solicitors to recommend your services. If you are sufficiently experienced you will have no trouble in obtaining work.

As a business consultant

To be a business consultant, by definition, you must have either qualifications or considerable experience in your field to justify charging for your time and advice. Again, your best market is likely to be the small business, which can employ you for a few hours each week and thus avoid needing an additional member of staff, with all the costs that involves. As with book-keeping, if you feel you have something to give the business world, contact your local banks, accountants and solicitors and make them aware of what you have to offer. Similarly, telephone your local Small Firms Information Service and the Department of Industry and try and persuade them to recommend you.

As a computer programmer

A great many software houses use freelance computer programmers working from home. Sometimes the software houses will provide the hardware, in other instances they expect a freelance to have her own equipment. Clearly you need to be experienced to offer this service and if you are, you should contact The Association of Independent Computer Specialists, Leicester House, 8 Leicester Street, London WC2H 7BN, who can provide you with a great deal of information.

As a gardener

If you enjoy gardening and working in the fresh air, why not offer your services as a freelance gardener. The advantage of this job is that it is relatively regular – lawns need cutting weekly, beds need clearing fortnightly. Once you have established a few clients, you can very easily find yourself in full-time work, and then you could employ an assistant. With the pressures on time that everyone seems to suffer these days, it is not difficult to find people who simply do not have enough hours in the day to mow their own lawns and prune their own roses. Advertise locally and I think you will be surprised by the response.

As a hairdresser

You need to be apprenticed and trained to be a hairdresser – the results of being too much of an amateur could be disastrous! You will not achieve, in an employment sense, the accolade of a major stylist unless you have been through a very long-winded programme of training and pecking orders, but once you are competent, there is nothing to stop you setting up on your own – either visiting people's houses or opening your own salon. There is a big market for travelling hairdressers, particularly amongst elderly people. Look carefully at what is needed in your area.

As an interpreter

If you have a fluent second language, there could well be opportunities for you to make money by using it. There are two main avenues – you can contact your local tourist board and see if there is any scope for being a curator or guide for foreign visitors, or you could contact The British Overseas Trade Board at 1 Victoria Street, London SW1, who handle a large number of enquiries from would-be exporters and who may be able to recommend your services. There is also the possibility of teaching English as a foreign language to students whose native tongue is your own second language – local colleges should be able to help you with this.

As a market researcher

There are quite a number of opportunities in market research. You need a car and a telephone and you must be prepared to work unsociable hours, such as evenings and weekends when most people are at home. Look up market research companies in your local Yellow Pages. If none are listed, try ringing local advertising agents for advice. There is nothing to stop you working for several market research companies at once. You need to like people and you need to be fairly thick-skinned as, for every person who enjoys being asked questions, there are several who consider it to be an invasion of privacy.

As a cleaner

Following the lead from America, there remains little or no stigma attached to being a domestic or office cleaner. Mrs Mops come from all walks of life these days. They often drive to work in their own cars and have as good, if not better standards of living than the people for whom they work. You should not feel degraded in any way by offering your services as a cleaner. Some people, by dint of choice or necessity, have to leave their home every day in order to go out to work. You, by the same dint of choice or necessity, are prepared to undertake the job of sorting the place out in their absence.

More people need cleaners than are ever available and there is no reason why you should not turn cleaning into a very successful business – becoming extremely fast and high-powered, tearing from house to house, using your own equipment and possibly employing several assistants as well. Look at the needs of your local area.

As a painter and decorator

You do not need any training as such. If you are a naturally good handywoman then there is absolutely no reason why you should not offer your painting and decorating skills for hire. There are tricks of the trade, however, and it is important you buy your paint at the right price but, frankly, as a woman, you have an enormous advantage. As I mentioned earlier with regard to odd jobbing, a woman is often more acceptable in and around a home than a man, and there is a lot of money to be made out of providing fast, efficient painting and decorating services. If you could apprentice yourself to a local decorator for a few months I think you would find this very helpful.

As a removals woman

You may say this is not a job for a woman, but there is nothing to stop you employing a few strong-armed men to help you. All you need is a second-hand van, an answering machine and, of course, you do need to be based in a fairly urban area. Removals are not just restricted to moving homes. People are always buying items that do not fit into their car and very often need delivery by the following day, or whatever. A trip around local auction rooms, furniture stores or garden centres, will bring you regular business and, certainly, if you are prepared to work evenings and weekends, you can compete with the 'big boys' in the moving of homes as well.

As a teacher

If you have a genuine fund of knowledge to offer, teaching is an excellent way of making money, since all you are selling is your time and your knowledge and there are usually precious few overheads. You can offer private tuition – helping children and young people to pass particular exams. You can teach in quite specific problem areas, such as dyslexia, blindness, deafness, mental or physical handicaps. You can give driving lessons, ballet and dance lessons, keep fit, yoga, languages, music, riding... you could even set up a correspondence course if your subject is sufficiently obscure that you need to pool pupils from all over the country. The possibilities are endless. Do you have anything to offer?

Answering telephones

A telephone answering service is a very useful thing to offer as an alternative to the telephone answering machines that we all hate so much. British Telecom have a really useful switching device so that your clients can have calls diverted to you when they are out and vice versa. It is a facility you can offer to a number of businesses, from a doctor's surgery to a busy plumber, to a mail-order company needing an extra line to take orders. Advertise in your local papers to obtain work.

As a translator

There is excellent potential for translating in Britain since most of us refuse to learn a second language! If you have a foreign language at your fingertips then there is always work as a translator. As with interpreting, contact the British Overseas Board, who should be able to advise you. If you are thinking of learning a language that could be useful commercially, consider Japanese, Russian or Arabic – you will be inundated with work if you can master one of these.

What to do with your home . . .

Bed and breakfast

To run a bed and breakfast establishment from your own home, you can only let 50 per cent of your accommodation, that is, if you have four bedrooms, you can let two. You cannot let guests sleep in the attic or in a basement and you have to make sure that there is an adequate means of escape in the event of fire. Legislation is only part of the picture, though. You really do have to like people, very much indeed, to be able to tolerate them within your own home. Obviously the better the facilities you can offer, the more you can charge and, particularly if you live in a tourist area, this can be a very lucrative way of making extra money.

Commercial use

It may be possible to use part of your home commercially – perhaps open an art gallery or run a shop or offer cream teas. There are endless possibilities but you do have to be careful about planning (more of this in Chapter 7). However, assuming you are happy to have the public in your home or garden, then look at what you have to offer and what the environment may need. It could mean that within your own four walls you are sitting on a gold mine.

Room or flat letting

The Department of Environment publishes a leaflet called 'Letting Rooms In Your Home', which is an extremely useful guide and will help to ensure that you do not encounter any legal difficulties. If you have a large house with room to spare, having a lodger can be an added bonus – provided you choose the right person. Great care must be taken in the selection of anyone to whom you let off part of your home. Money is important, of course, but in some respects too much emphasis is placed on the ability of someone to pay the rent – what is important is that you can live with them. Foreign students can often be a good source of income, provided you really do have the time to be a proxy mum and show them around the area – in other words you must be sure they get their money's worth. Usually, it is preferable if you have children of a similar age, so that they can all entertain one another.

Speculation

In buying, selling and converting property, fortunes have been made... and lost. If you have spare capital, then from the comfort of your own home you can buy a property, get builders to work on it and hopefully sell it at a vast profit a couple of years later. However, I would not advise you to become involved in property conversion, outside that of your own home, if you have to borrow money, for the combination of the Capital Gains Tax you will have to pay and bank interest can often make the most promising enterprise extremely unprofitable.

The alternative, of course, is to trade up in your own home. Sell your house, buy a bigger one, renovate it and sell it a couple of years later... and then move on again. This way, of course, you avoid Capital Gains Tax and, if you have the stamina, it could prove to be a very lucrative business. Provided you make no serious mistakes, you simply move on every two or three years, either getting a bigger and better house each time or buying a similar but run-down property so that your improvements turn themselves into cash in the bank. Obviously the more renovation work you can actually tackle yourself, the more profit you will make. However, so far as family life is concerned, it is enormously disruptive. It is said that moving house is one of the greatest traumas any of us have to face and, certainly, if you have young children, you are putting an awful lot of stress on the family.

What you could do with your garden...

Breeding and rearing

You could breed bees, goats, pedigree dogs and cats, parrots, ducks, horses... There are endless possibilities for breeding birds and animals, particularly if you have a fair amount of space. The chief problem, however, is the difficulty of being a commercial success where birds and animals are concerned and it is important to recognize that this sort of pursuit is more likely to be a hobby, which hopefully will pay for itself, rather than a money-making scheme. If you are looking at trying to make money out of the breeding of birds or animals, do concentrate on rare breeds as the price for the offspring is likely to exceed the cost involved in breeding them.

Camping and caravans

If you live in a suitable part of the country and have sufficient land, it may be possible to let off some of it as a camping or caravan site. You will receive good money for offering little more than a field and some form of cold, running water. In addition, there is a subsidiary income to be made by selling farm produce to the campers. It could be the most profitable crop you have ever had!

Grow herbs

If you have a reasonable patch of garden, why not consider growing herbs? There is an increasing demand for herbs, both for culinary use and for medicinal purposes with the growing interest in alternative medicine. Why not visit your local health food shop and discuss what herbs are most in demand. You do not need to grow a whole variety – you could specialize in one or two, which you could sell to wholesalers without involving any costs of packaging or marketing.

Open your garden to the public

If you live in a delightful area, which also happens to attract tourists, you could consider opening your garden to the public. This does not necessarily mean you have to offer refreshments, although obviously it would provide an additional source of income. If you can cultivate a truly spectacular garden (and it does not need to be a large one) you will find that the public will flock to it. All that will be required of you is to explain how you have done it! You could consider selling cuttings and bedding plants to boost the income.

Have a market garden

The National Farmers' Union, Agriculture House, Knightsbridge, London SW1, have a horticultural section that will be able to give you some advice on market gardening. The last thing you want to do is to grow potatoes, carrots and other basic fare – you want to aim for exotic vegetables and flowers so you lessen your competition. In order to establish what is most likely to sell, visit garden centres and ask them what they want. If you have any running water on your land, aquatic plants are becoming increasingly popular and, as mentioned previously, there is a big market for herbs. Certainly do not grow onions where you could grow asparagus! Look, too, at the increasing interest in organic produce – again the NFU will be able to give advice on preparation of soil and suitable produce to grow.

How are you at selling . . .

On a market stall

For just a few pounds a week, you can acquire a market stall in your local market town. You can then sell your own produce or other people's. Good trade is done in end-of-line goods and rejects from factories or you can emulate the Women's Institute and offer home-made pies, cakes and preserves. Prices have to be low though, people do expect bargains on a market stall.

Via a party plan

Tupperware is probably the most famous name here, but there are a number of established firms who are seeking people to help with their party selling. Write to the Direct Selling Association, 44 Russell Square, London WC1B 4JP. They have a leaflet stating the code of practice for in-home selling that you will find useful if you want to start up your own party plan – otherwise contact one of the major companies in the business and see what they have to offer.

Door-to-door

This is the tough end of selling. If you are really good, it can be extremely lucrative – whether it is insurance, double glazing, encyclopaedias or something more original. You can develop a very personal technique and certainly, here again, I think being a woman is an advantage since people will be marginally less rude to you than they would to a man – and less suspicious. You need a car and a telephone, a cast-iron constitution and a sturdy ego. You will have no difficulty in finding a freelance selling job as they are offered in newspapers every day of the week. The trick, of course, is to find one where you actually stand a chance of making money! If the company in whom you are interested is worth dealing with at all, they will allow you to speak to one or two established freelance salesmen to see how they are getting on and to substantiate the claims of potential income. If they expect you to buy *any* equipment, it is a con. Steer well clear – truly.

On the telephone

Employment agencies are most likely to be able to find you telephone selling jobs. Obviously you need a clear, pleasant, friendly speaking voice and you will also need a second telephone installed in your house to separate the business calls from the household ones. You will be expected to pay for the use of the telephone out of your earnings, so you could lose a lot of money if you are not successful. Do bear this in mind.

Are you a caring person?

Home-help service

The DHSS provide a good home-help service for the elderly, those recovering from an illness or for women with small children who cannot cope. The home-help service provides cleaning, shopping and a minor degree of nursing care, so that, in many instances, no actual training is needed. Contact your local DHSS for details.

Childminding, nannying or companion to the sick or elderly

You can register through the DHSS as an official childminder. You need to offer adequate facilities and you will almost certainly receive a visit from a local social worker from time to time, to ensure that the facilities you have available are up to scratch. Alternatively, of course, you can come to a private arrangement to look after someone's child, though if you are looking after a child who is not a relative of yours for more than two hours a day, you should register with the DHSS.

Apart from full-time nannying, there are many lucrative services to be offered, such as collecting children from school, giving them tea and seeing to their homework before their working mother returns. This could also include looking after children during the school holidays when both parents are committed to work.

As we all live longer these days, care of the elderly is an increasing problem. If you enjoy the company of older people, you could be a home-help and/or companion to one or more in your area – coming to a private arrangement rather than operating through the DHSS.

The bible for all forms of homecare is *The Lady*, which extensively advertises requirements in the homehelp field.

The home worker . . .

A number of traditional industries offer piecemeal work for people (usually women) to undertake in the home. Traditionally these jobs are very badly paid. Normally the company supplies the basic raw material to the home worker one week and the following week collects the finished goods, whatever they may be. The home worker is paid only for that part of her work that is considered to be satisfactory. Anything that is considered substandard is returned and has to be put right. In the past there has been no question of sick pay, holiday pay or, indeed, any recognition of employee status and, in many instances, things have changed not at all. To understand your rights contact the Department of Employment, Wages Information,
17 Red Lion Square, London WC1R 4NH, and ask for their booklet on The Wages Council Act. There is a lot of work available in this field, particularly in rural areas but do be wary of being exploited.

These then represent the main areas of potential small business activity. I hope this chapter will have given you some ideas.

As a woman, do consider the possibility of competing with men at their own game. Take painting and decorating or perhaps window cleaning – the novelty of being a woman will make people remember you – and the fact that you are almost certain to do a better, neater job than a man!

5 Financing your business

Finding the necessary finance is always considered to be the major stumbling block in starting a business venture. This is not the case, *provided you go about it in the right way*. Careful planning is needed to ensure that not only do you have the right *amount* of finance, but also the right *type* and that there is sufficient flexibility in your financial planning to allow for both the lean times and a sudden upsurge in business. Too much borrowing can be as much of a disaster as being underfinanced. Many a potentially good business fails, not from lack of sales or skill and commitment on behalf of the principal, but from nothing more or less than the problem of cash flow. Let us look at how you should tackle the financial implications of your proposed business venture.

Assessing your financial requirements

Before you can begin to name the sum of money you will require to start your own business, you must first sit down and undertake a detailed analysis of precisely where you see your business going. This means you will have to forecast what you expect to achieve, at any rate for the first 12 months of operation and, if possible, for the first two years. 'This is impossible', you may say, 'how can I possibly know how many enamelled boxes I will be able to sell over a 12-month period?' The answer to this is to adopt a positive attitude.

Let us take the example of a would-be enameller. She is going to have to commit herself to the buying of a kiln and equipment, raw materials and possibly pay for a course. She may be having to purchase and build a workshop and, above all, she is going to have to commit hours and hours of potential money-making time to her scheme. This being the case, the initial question she should be asking herself is not so much how many boxes do I *think* I can sell, but how many boxes *must* I sell in order to justify the whole operation. This basic 'back of an envelope' calculation as to how many sales you must make to have a viable business is the most vital part of your whole forecasting operation. You are in business to sell something – whether it be a product or a service and, unless you can satisfy yourself that you really can sell what you intend to produce, then do not commit yourself to any major form of financing. You have to believe in the potential of your market. If you are so lacking in confidence that you cannot name a figure of what you earnestly believe you can sell in the next 12 months, then it is better to start your money-making scheme as a hobby – in which case the minimum of capital should be employed in it. However, let us be constructive and assume that you can see the shape of sales for the next 12 to 24 months. What you now have to do is to prepare a Profit Plan and a Cash Forecast.

The Profit Plan is just what it says and is the first part of the forecasting operation. Assuming you sell X and it costs Y to produce, involving Z people, will you have a profit when you have taken Y and Z away from the revenue from X? The second part of the equation is the Cash Forecast, which is a natural progression from the Profit Plan. Having worked out your plan over 12 months, you should then translate it into cash terms to see how much money you are going to need in order to generate your planned profit. It sounds complicated but really it is extremely easy. You will see, on the following pages, I have produced both a mock-up Profit Plan and Cash Forecast for you to study. Let me take you through the preparation of each.

A profit plan

Prepare a chart, as indicated, with 12 monthly columns for the first year of your trading, plus an additional column for the year's total. You do not need to start your chart at the beginning of the calendar year – work on the 12 months from the month in which you first start trading.

The first figure you need to put in is the sales figure we have discussed, plotting it over the next 12 months, on a month by month basis. Remember to take account of seasonal trends. Will you sell more or fewer over the Christmas period, more or fewer over the summer holidays? If you are going to register for VAT and charge VAT on your goods, the sales figures in your plan will need to be shown *net* of VAT.

The next stage is to calculate your *direct costs* on those sales. If you are registered for VAT, deduct the VAT element from your direct costs, for you will be able to reclaim the VAT paid. If you are not going to be registered for VAT then your direct costs must include the VAT element.

If your business simply involves the buying in and selling on of goods, then direct costs are simply the purchase price of these goods. If you are going to manufacture goods, then the direct costs will consist of two elements – the cost of all your raw materials and the cost of the labour needed to manufacture the goods.

This kind of labour is known as *direct labour*. A quick note on labour here. You should only show as a direct cost the wages of yourself or any staff you may have, who are *actively involved* in the manufacturing process. Indirect labour should not be included as a direct cost. What do I mean by *indirect labour* – secretaries, accountants, the receptionist, drivers, the boy who helps out in the warehouse – these are all indirect labour costs and part of your general overheads.

If you are selling a service, then all that is involved is your time, in which case your direct costs are nil. Some businesses are further complicated by the fact that they may consist of several different types of trading. An advertising agency, for example, may run a marketing consultancy service as well as booking space in national newspapers, which they then sell on to their clients. This will involve them in one set of sales with no direct costs and one set of sales with considerable direct costs. The only way to show this on a Profit Plan is to split the sales and apply the relevant costs accordingly.

Having established your direct costs, you should then take them away from your sales figure, again on a month by month basis, and what you are left with is the *gross profit*.

Once you have your *gross profit* figure, the final step is to deduct your overheads in order to establish a *net profit*, and here it is very important to ensure that you include every item of cost. You will see on the Profit Plan I have laid out the basic elements of cost you are likely to incur. In a Profit Plan it is important that you take your annual costs and split them equally over 12 months. For example, whilst you may only pay rent every quarter, the cost element of your rent should be shown on a monthly basis. Similarly with insurance, where the premium is likely to be paid annually, this should be split so it appears on a month by month basis, so that each month's sales attracts its true proportion of overheads. This means that many of

	Oct	Nov	Dec	Jan	Feb	March	April	May	June	July	Aug	Sept	Annual Total
Sales (net of VAT)													
Less, direct costs: material labour													
Gross profit													
Rent													
Rates													
Light and heat													
Repairs and Maintenance													
Staff wages, including National Insurance and PAYE contributions (Indirect costs)													
Travel expenses													
Telephone and post													
Printing and stationery													
Legal and professional													
Insurance													
Advertising													
Bank interest and charges													
Depreciation													
Total overheads													
Net profit (loss)													

	Oct	Nov	Dec	Jan	Feb	March	April	May	June	July	Aug	Sept	Annual Total
Sales – cash													
Sales – credit													
Other receipts													
VAT refunds													
Total receipts													
Capital expenditure													
Rent													
Rates													
Light and heat													
Repairs and maintenance													
Staff wages – both direct and indirect (NB note on PAYE and NI)													
Raw materials													
Travel expenses													
Telephone and post													
Printing and stationery													
Legal and professional													
Insurance													
Advertising													
Bank interest and charges													
VAT payments													
Other payments													
Total payments													
Cash in (out) – for month													
Cash balance (overdraft)													

the overhead costs will remain the same for each month, though others, obviously, like light and heat, will increase in the winter, while travel expenses, telephone, post, printing and stationery will be liable to fluctuations according to how much business you are doing.

Do not worry if in some months – particularly the early months of the business – you are making quite a substantial loss. Few businesses, even well-established ones, are profitable *every* month. You also need to recognize that very many businesses make no profit at all in the first year or even two years of trading. This, too, does not matter, provided it has been catered for. This indeed is the object of the plan. Not only does it help you assess the viability of your business, but it will also show you how long it will take you to build it into a profitable one. It is very difficult to generalize, but if you can demonstrate to yourself that the last three to four months of your first year are showing a profit and your annual profit/loss figure comes out at about break even, then, in my view, you have the makings of a very successful business.

A cash forecast

A cash forecast is easier to prepare than a profit plan because you have already made all the calculations of your sales and costs. Now it is simply a question of expressing the calculations in a different way. You will see from the chart that we have headed it up again with the 12 months and annual total. The object of a cash forecast is to see the pattern of your sales and expenses so that you can judge how much money you are going to need in any one month.

A general note on cash forecasting: whether or not you are registered for VAT, all your items of sales and expenses should *include* VAT for the purpose of cash forecasting, because this is the figure you actually pay out or receive in. You will see however that there are two items listed for VAT – repayments and payments – where you will enter the money you pay out or receive from the VAT office as it falls due (more on VAT in the next chapter).

The first item you enter on your cash forecast is, again, sales but this time you need to reflect on the nature of your sales. Are your sales paid for in cash only or are you offering credit? For the purposes of a cash forecast, *sales can only be entered when the money is likely to be received*. If you are running a shop, then clearly most of your transactions are likely to be in cash. However, if you are supplying goods to a wholesaler, you may well offer credit terms, in which case you have to calculate when you should receive payment and only enter the sale as a sale at the time of receipt of a cheque. You will see I have shown two elements of sales – both cash and credit – since you may well have a mix of both.

You should then allow a line for *other receipts*, which literally will include anything else you receive in an income or capital sense. You might get a cash bonus from your supplier for a big order or receive agency commissions, or you may sell a piece of equipment or sub-let part of your premises – in other words any receipt that is neither a sale nor a VAT refund should go into other receipts. Finally, as already discussed, there is a line for VAT refunds. Once you have listed all your receipts for the month, these should then be totalled and entered in *total receipts*.

The next item you will see on the cash forecast is *capital expenditure*, and this entry is liable to apply particularly in the early days of a business. If we use the example of the enameller once again, the purchase of a kiln, equipment and a workshop would be put here. It is important to emphasize at this point the difference between the profit plan and the cash forecast. In the profit plan you are concerned with profit and, therefore, other than allowing for the depreciation of your assets, capital expenditure is not in itself relevant. In the cash forecast you are simply trying to assess how much money you need to run your business and therefore capital expenditure is very relevant.

After capital expenditure you will see I have listed virtually the same overheads as for the profit plan. Staff wages no longer need to be split between direct and indirect and there is an additional column for VAT payments.

The way to compete the cash forecast is to fill in the same figures as on the profit plan but this time apply them to *the month in which you actually make the payment*. Back to the example of rent – if you pay your rent quarterly, now you need to show it as a quarterly payment rather than a monthly allocation. If you receive credit terms from your supplier, then you need to show the purchase of materials, not necessarily pro rata with the sales you have made in the same month, but reflecting the fact that you have received a month's credit. This, of course, amply demonstrates the huge advantage of receiving credit and giving none! If you make big cash sales in February but do not have to pay for your raw materials until March, there will be an upsurge in your cash balance. If, on the other hand, you have to pay cash for your raw materials and give credit to your customers, then February is going to show a fairly hefty overdraft. Similarly, if you need to build up stock in expectation of sales, this will reflect itself in the cash you will need to pay out on those purchases. This is what the cash forecast is all about – demonstrating the movement of money.

An important point to note on wages: actual staff wages should be applied to the month in which they are paid, but PAYE and national insurance (which together represent approximately 30 per cent of the total wage bill) do not have to be paid until the month following your payment to staff. This means that 70 per cent of your wage bill should be shown in the month in which it falls due and 30 per cent should be carried forward to the following month. All other items of expenditure – bank interest and charges, legal and professional fees, advertising and insurance should only be shown in the month in which you actually have to make payment.

Having reallocated these overheads you should then total them to include the capital expenditure. You will then have two figures – your total receipts for the month and your total payments. If payments exceed receipts then clearly they are going to have to be funded. It is this fluctuating bottom line that forms the basis of your calculations as to how much finance you are actually going to need, month by month.

I cannot stress how important it is to take time and trouble to ensure that both your profit plan and cash forecast are as accurate as possible. We will now look at how to finance your business but, before doing so, I would ask you to consider, the justification for the figures you have produced. Above all, do not delude yourself and dress up the figures to look better. The only person who will suffer in those circumstances will be you. Of course you have to take an optimistic line – unless you are enthusiastic and believe in what you are doing then there is no point in going into business at all. However, do temper your optimism with realism.

Conversely, just because your business is going to make a loss in the first year and therefore during that first 12 months of operation the cash goes only one way – OUT! – it does not mean that you cannot go on to be highly successful. Where you will fail is if you convince yourself – and your bank manager – that you are going to move into profit long before you actually do. Planned borrowing and planned losses are perfectly acceptable to financial institutions because everyone knows that this is a recognized part of the birth and growing pains of a business. However, without a plan, a sudden increase in overdraft and a continuing pattern of losses will send your financial backer into a blind panic. This could result in a totally unjustified action to wind up your business, when a few more months of trading could see you romping home with record profits. So, do not doctor the figures or you will be on to a hiding to nothing.

Borrowing money – sources of finance

Having completed your profit plan and cash forecast, you may well have thrown up a requirement for capital that you personally do not have. In these circumstances, you either have to borrow it or find some other method of raising it. In this section we are looking quite specifically at *borrowing money*.

The borrowing of money for a small business falls into two categories – borrowing from banks or borrowing from other sources. Let us look first at banks.

Banks

It is a popular misconception that banks have money available to invest in commercial enterprises. Essentially this is not true, for it is not a bank's job to provide any form of permanent capital in a business. In other words it is no good going to a bank and saying that you need £5,000 to start a business, without demonstrating how this money is going to be repaid. This, of course, is where the profit plan and cash forecast come into their own. A bank is prepared to lend money in two ways – either by way of a loan, usually over five to ten years, for the purpose of a quite specific purchase, such as a property or equipment – provided that that loan is to be repaid on a monthly reducing basis, over the period in question. Alternatively, or in addition, banks are prepared to support day-to-day trading by means of an overdraft facility, to help you even out the peaks and troughs of your cash flow. This being the case, you may well persuade a bank to, say, lend you £3,000 – £4,000 to purchase your equipment and to grant you an additional £1,000 overdraft, having carefully examined your cash forecast and seen that this is how much you will need to finance your heaviest month of expenditure.

Your whole approach will be made very much easier if you can invest any of your own personal money in your business venture. Certainly there are very few banks who will not match your own investment – in other words if you are putting in £1,000 and have a reasonable banking record, you can be assured that a bank will match your figure with another £1,000. However, if you have absolutely no capital of your own, there is still no reason why you should not be able to borrow money, but you will have to ensure that your presentation is slick.

Government guaranteed loan scheme

This scheme is available to proprietors of new and existing small businesses and is working very well. If you find resistance from your bank to lend you the money you require, because you cannot offer any security, it is well worth suggesting to them that they consider the Government Guaranteed Loan Scheme.

This is how it works. If you wish to raise a sum of money and neither have any capital of your own nor any security to offer the bank, under the scheme, the Government provides the bank with security by guaranteeing 70 per cent of the loan, provided that the bank is prepared to risk the remaining 30 per cent. This, of course, greatly minimizes the bank's risk, but whether you are eligible for the Government Guaranteed Loan Scheme or not, still depends entirely on your ability to persuade the bank manager as to the viability of your business.

Let us look at presentation for a moment. In theory, it is a good idea to first approach your own existing bankers. They know you, they know your family circumstances and, whilst this may work against you, it could work for you. However, if you live in a small town and you want to borrow a fairly substantial sum of money (say, £10,000) it might be sensible to consider approaching a major branch in a big city. The reason for this is that the bank manager in a big branch has a personal limit of borrowing that will be far in excess of your small town man. From experience, when you are trying to sell an idea, it is far better to sell to the man who is going to make the decision, than have your proposal sent up to Head Office for approval. Also, a big branch is more used to handling large sums of money. Your £10,000 overdraft, in a small branch, stands out like a sore thumb. In a major city branch, it is just one of the herd. The problem, of course, with applying to a brand new bank is that the first question asked will be why you have not approached your own bank. For this reason, if at all possible, try and obtain a personal introduction to a major bank. If successful in this, your answer can be, 'Because my solicitor, Mr Bloggs, suggested I made contact with you as you are particularly experienced in dealing with new businesses.'

When approaching a bank, do marshall your facts together very carefully. In addition to your Cash Forecast and Profit Plan, you need as much documentation and general business memorabilia as possible. So far as documentation is concerned, if you have any orders or letters from satisfied customers, or write-ups in newspapers, bring the whole lot along to the meeting. If you are going to be selling a product, if humanly possible, bring the product too. Bank managers love to feel and touch something solid! Photostat everything and leave a complete set with him – this demonstrates efficiency. Most important: for heavens sake, be nothing less than wildly enthusiastic, carrying him along with the excitement of the whole venture.

A natural question arises here as to whether women are at a disadvantage when it comes to borrowing money, and I have to say that in the initial stages they are. In this book, I have fallen into the trap of calling the bank manager 'he' because, almost always, still, bank managers are men. I have known some wonderful bank managers in my commercial dealings but they can be a slightly pompous, intimidating bunch at times, and none of us likes having to go cap in hand to ask for something. You will find that they have a tendency to talk down to you and you must not allow yourself to feel intimidated by this. You are as good as they are. Make sure they know it and never, never deal with anybody other than the branch manager – do not be fobbed off with one of his assistants.

A case history *I have a great buddy called Elsa, who used to work for a major American merchant bank. She is a very high-powered lady and has spent a great deal of her working life jet-setting backwards and forwards across the Atlantic. After a number of years of this, she felt she needed a change and decided to start her own property agency. She did her Profit Plan and Cash Forecast and then went along to her bank manager with a modest requirement for £5,000. The manager was young and fairly chinless and started lecturing her about how the bank was not in the business of lending risk money. Elsa had been used to dealing in millions of dollars and is well-known for her volatility. In a fit of rage she stood up, leaned across the desk, grabbed the poor little man by his tie and pulled him to his feet. 'Look, Buddy', she said, 'up until a few weeks ago I was employing little jerks like you. Now are you going to lend me the money or are you going to miss the opportunity of a lifetime?'*

She got her overdraft!

The others

Banks are not the only source for borrowing money. Let us look at the other main avenues available.

The Enterprise Allowance Scheme

The Enterprise Allowance Scheme is designed to help people during the first 12 months of their business. To qualify for the scheme, you must be between the ages of 18 and retirement and have received unemployment benefit or supplementary benefit, as a result of being out of work, for at least eight weeks. In addition, you must be able to demonstrate that you can invest a minimum of £1,000 in your business, but this money does not need to be your own – you can raise it by means of a loan or an overdraft. If you do qualify, you will receive £40 a week for 52 weeks, which can be a great help in the early days. Contact your local job centre for details.

Investors in industry (3i)

An independent commercial body, 3i, was formed by the bank of England and the major clearing banks. The aim of 3i is to provide permanent finance to encourage the growth and development of small and medium-sized businesses. They will loan as little as £5,000 and up to as much as £2,000,000 and, preferably, they like to be involved in the inception of a business. However, if your ambitions are small and you have no particular inclination to expand beyond a cottage industry-type of operation, then 3i is not for you. They are ambitious for their clients and like to feel that they are investing in companies that are 'going places'. If you do have great plans for your business, however, they are excellent people to deal with. They take a share in the equity of the company, but not a large shareholding and, provided that your business does not get into severe financial trouble, they interfere not at all. Your local bank manager will advise you as to the nearest 3i office.

The Council for Small Industries in Rural Areas (CoSIRA)

CoSIRA as the name suggests concentrates on assisting businesses in country districts. This does not mean, however, that their main aim is to support picturesque craft industries. They are interested in any form of business enterprise and can help with small grants or loans. Their head office is at 141 Castle Street, Salisbury, Wiltshire SP1 3TP (telephone 0772 336225) and there are regional offices around the country.

Small firms division

The Department of Industry has what is called a small firms division and their head office is at Abell House, John Islip Street, London SW1 (telephone 01-212 3395). Here again, the small firms division have regional offices and some areas do have some funding available. Contact your regional office and ask for details.

Your local authority

Some areas of the country have been designated as development areas where

69

money is being channelled in quite specifically to help encourage the development of private enterprise. Even if you are not in a development area, it may well be that your Local Authority can give you some form of assistance, particularly when it comes to subsidized industrial premises. To benefit from Local Authority help you do need a fairly imaginative scheme that is going to mean employment for local people. In any event, contact them and see what is available.

Tourism

If your money-making scheme is aimed at the tourist, it may well be that The Tourist Board can help you with funding. In England and Wales there is funding available for specific tourist projects, of up to £100,000, and the Scottish Tourist Board are also susceptible to ideas for improving tourist amenities. You can contact these Tourist Boards at the following addresses:

English Tourist Board, Thames Tower, Blacks Road, London W69 E1
Telephone: 01-846 9000

Wales Tourist Board, Brunnell House, 2 Fitzalan Road, Cardiff CF2 1UY
Telephone: 0222 499909

Scottish Tourist Board, 23 Ravelston Terrace, Edinburgh EH4 3EU
Telephone: 031 332 2433

Business Expansion Scheme

You are likely to have heard quite a lot about the Business Expansion Scheme in the media. It is a good scheme because everyone wins. It offers the high income earner the opportunity to avoid tax legally, by investing in UK-based trading companies. The investor can subscribe up to £40,000 in any one year and can claim the total sum as a deduction from normal taxable income. The minimum amount of money the investor can put into a company is £500, and it has to be invested for a minimum of five years.

There are a number of exceptions. BES schemes are not available to property companies (other than those specializing in providing rented residential accommodation), hire-purchase companies, insurance, accountancy, legal services, banking, leasing and the farming trade, but most manufacturing and service industries *are* eligible.

Recently an adjunct to the BES scheme has developed in the form of BES funds. Stock brokers and insurance companies have started to get together a number of companies requiring BES money and forming a portfolio. Clients are then offered the opportunity of investing in the fund as a whole, rather than in the individual companies, thus spreading the risk. If you feel you might be eligible for BES funding, discuss it with your bank manager, any rich friends you might have and your accountant. It would be worth approaching any stock brokers, merchant banks or insurance companies, where you have a contact, to see if they run BES Funds.

The big time

It is often said that it is far easier to borrow vast sums of money than it is to borrow a few thousand and, certainly, if your money-making scheme requires big money, that is £250,000 or more, then it is worth considering insurance companies, pension funds, merchant banks or possibly even 'going public'. Within the confines of this book, it does not seem sensible to go into great detail on how to acquire big money, for every business is different and, in any event, you will need the professional advice of accountants and solicitors, before even contemplating such a step. If you are ambitious though, here is a carrot – once you have a profitable, proven company, taking it up the next rung of the ladder is a great deal easier than being the chief attendant at its birth.

How not to borrow money

Any relatively self-reliant articulate woman, who believes in her project and wants to borrow money to finance it, can always do so. What you have to consider is whether you are *wise* to do so. There are a number of ways of financing your business without committing yourself to borrowing so let us look at these.

Partners

In Chapter 8, we will be dealing in detail with the mechanics of joining forces with a partner so let us just look at this option briefly here. There is no point in taking on a partner, absolutely no point in sharing the profits, unless your partner is going to contribute something. It could be skill or hard work or, alternatively, it could be good old-fashioned cash. There are a variety of reasons why someone might want to become your partner and help finance your business. It could be that they have a high income and want to reduce their tax burden (see Business Expansion Scheme), it could be that they have time on their hands and want an interest, it could be that they believe your idea is so brilliant that they want part of the action – or perhaps they just like you. Carefully constructed, a business partnership can be very successful but do be wary of the sleeping partner who has no role in your business other than lending you money. In the early stages, you will be enormously grateful to the person who has financed your business and has made it all possible. Obviously your partner is going to want some sort of return for lending you money, which is likely to be expressed in terms of a share in the profits. However, your unswerving gratitude, after three or four years of hard grind, may turn to resentment when you find that your partner is still enjoying, say, 40 per cent of the profits of a now rapidly expanding business, in which he or she is doing no work at all and in which *you* are having to cope with every imaginable headache. In these circumstances, you have to remember that you would have no business at all without your partner. However, in striking any deal with a partner, it is sensible to look ahead and make sure that you can cope with the implications.

Hire-purchase and leasing

Rather than purchase the equipment you need, you could consider buying it on hire-purchase or, perhaps, leasing it. This is an expensive method of finance but it can be useful in the early days of a business, if you are not sure how much, or even what equipment you need. Most hire-purchase and leasing companies will be prepared to swop around the types of equipment you need, under the terms of trade, particularly if you are trading upwards into more exotic requirements. However, once you have bought something outright it is more difficult to realize the investment if you find at a later date you have made a mistake. Maybe you could finance your business by a mix comprising a small investment of your own, a working overdraft and the hire-purchase of your equipment.

Suppliers' credit

Particularly where you are dealing with one or two major suppliers, you might be able to persuade them to give you extended credit – say 60 days instead of 30. Of course this means you will receive no discounts but it is likely to be a far cheaper method of finance than borrowing an equivalent sum from a bank. What, of course, you have to demonstrate to your suppliers is that your credit-worthiness is sufficient to make such a proposition attractive. It depends how badly the suppliers want your business, but why not ask – be cheeky, you have nothing to lose.

Payments on account from customers

The reverse of suppliers' credit is to ask customers for payment in advance, or at any rate, part payment. In some industries it is standard procedure and, certainly, if you are undertaking an order for anything other than a purely standard stock item, you are perfectly entitled to ask for a payment on account. If your business involves the production of an individual requirement, payment on account should be your standard form of trading. Even a deposit, of 10 to 15 per cent, can have a dramatic effect on cash flow as, particularly in work-intensive craft industries, such a payment pays for the raw materials. A 50 per cent advance payment with your customer's order is not unrealistic, and can substantially fund your business.

Investing your own money

The most obvious alternative to borrowing money is to invest your own. You could take out a second mortgage on your house, sell Great Aunt Margaret's pearls, cash in your savings or even consider something really drastic like trading down into a smaller house or altering your lifestyle dramatically so as to generate cash. There are advantages in using your own money. It is usually cheaper and certainly demonstrates to your bankers, your suppliers, your customers, your landlord and your staff – where applicable – that you have confidence in what you are doing, and this in turn will tend to encourage their support. A word of warning, though. If you are intending to invest your own money in your business, then do view it in a strictly professional way. Bankers and private investors expect a return on the money they invest, and so should you. Of course you may feel justified in giving yourself a breathing space in the first few months of trading, but whatever investment you make has got to pay its way. You must do a deal with yourself to ensure that, say, in the case of a second mortgage, you are receiving interest on the money you have invested in your business that at least covers the mortgage repayments and, in the case of Great Aunt Margaret's pearl money, over, say, a five-year period, you should receive dividends at least on a par to what you could expect from putting the money on deposit in a bank.

Hopefully this chapter will have given you food for thought on how to finance your own money-making scheme. I cannot stress enough the need to be realistic in the financing of your business. Everything you undertake in the early days is likely to be more difficult than you had anticipated. Orders are slower, customers take longer to pay, there are hidden costs you had not even considered, you hit manufacturing snags... Do allow a little slack in your financing for the teething troubles that, in the early days of business, inevitably will be yours.

6 Taxation and social security

Everyone in the country is entitled to some free income

No book on any form of commercial enterprise would be complete without looking at taxation and its implications. How you are taxed is important and you also need to understand how tax affects your potential employees, if you intend taking on staff. It is a grizzly subject but please bear with me and battle through it, for it is vitally important that you use the system to best possible advantage. Earning a living is hard enough without running the risk of paying unnecessary tax.

Income tax

Everyone in the country – man, woman and child, is entitled to receive a level of income without having to pay any income tax. This tax-free income is secured by giving *personal allowances* of one sort or another, which ensure that the first few thousand pounds we earn are exempt from tax deduction.

It is important to understand what is meant by the term 'income'. Income is not simply wages – it represents virtually any form of money coming in, whether it be interest on money deposited in a bank, a pension, unemployment benefit, dividend or investment earnings. All of this is classified as income and once the total exceeds your personal allowance and any further allowable costs then it is subject to income tax.

For easy reference, the scale of personal allowances (1988–89) is as follows, but I would suggest you check these figures with your local tax office at the time of reading this book, since they are usually changed each year.

Single person's allowance or wife's earning allowance	£2,605
Married person's allowance	£4,095
Additional allowance for single-parent families/widows	£1,490
Age allowance (where either spouse is over 65):	
Single person's	£3,180
Married couple's	£5,035
Age allowance (where either spouse is over 80):	
Single person's	£3,310
Married couple's	£5,205

The age allowance is available if either you or your husband is over retirement age, but is an alternative to the normal personal allowance – not additional to it. It is reduced if your taxable income exceeds £10,600. The reduction is two-thirds of any income over £10,600 until the allowance equals the standard personal allowance.

In addition to these allowances, a number of other costs can be deducted from your gross income to arrive at taxable income. In the main, these are:

- interest on mortgages or loans used to purchase your only or main residence. Tax relief is available on loans of up to £30,000
- interest on mortgages or loans used to purchase or improve property that is available for letting throughout the year and is actually let for at least 26 weeks each year
- Business Expansion Scheme investments of up to £40,000
- premiums paid to approved pension schemes or for personal pension policies
- expenses necessary for you to carry out your work, such as travel and hotel costs (this does not include travel between work and home or entertaining)
- professional fees and subscriptions linked to your work
- if you are a sole trader or in

partnership – all business overheads and expenses.

The rates of income tax payable on taxable income for 1988–89 are:

- basic rate on first £19,300   25 per cent
- top rate on income over £19,300   40 per cent

Let us look at the status of a married woman in connection with income tax. Firstly a woman is treated as married if she *is* married and she *is* living with her husband. In most marriages, a man and his wife are taxed on their joint income – this includes their earnings, investment income and capital gains. However, the tax payable is actually assessed on the husband. This being the case, in a marriage where both husband and wife are earning, the practical effect is that the husband normally fills in the tax return, if he is sent the form by the tax office, and he pays Income Tax by way of PAYE on his earnings, while his wife pays PAYE on hers.

Two variations from the normal pattern are possible:

Wife's earnings election

This is separate taxation of a wife's earnings (this applies to earnings only and not to investment income or capital gains). A wife can elect to be taxed separately from her husband and, assuming they both have a high income, this can be a distinct advantage. What it means is that the couple are taxed virtually as though they were two single people, which means they each pay tax at 25 per cent on the first £19,300 of taxable income. If, for a moment, you look at a situation where a couple are each earning £19,300 but have not elected to be taxed separately, taxed jointly, the second £19,300 would attract an average tax of nearly 40 per cent. In these circumstances, separate taxation makes a lot of sense. However, it does have to be remembered that the moment a husband and wife opt for separate tax assessment, the husband loses the married couples' allowance, which, in effect, reduces his personal allowance by £1,490. As a quick rule of thumb, you need to have a joint income of about £28,500, of which the wife is earning at least £7,000 in order to justify being taxed separately.

Separate assessment

Either husband or wife can ask to have separate dealings with the Inland Revenue, so that each may submit his or her own Tax Return. This will not alter the total tax payable by the couple, but the Inspector of Taxes will calculate the figure and apportion the total tax in proportion to the husband and wife's individual incomes and make two separate assessments.

In the 1988 Budget, it was

announced that the whole of the current tax system, so far as it relates to the treatment of married women, will be reformed. As from 6 April 1990, a new system will be introduced to provide for independent taxation of the incomes of husbands and wives. This will give privacy for married women in their tax affairs, and independent taxation of capital gains. The new system will give full personal allowance for a married woman, a new married couples allowance and higher allowances for elderly wives.

Under the current political climate in this country, the gradual lowering of the top rates of income tax over recent years has made it increasingly attractive to strive for a high income. However, the way the system works, the higher the earnings the more, proportionally, you have to pay in income tax. If, therefore, you have your own business, it is sensible to keep your earnings as low as possible and maximize the expenses you can charge against your business. Do not go mad – Tax Inspectors are no fools and you simply cannot go charging everything under the sun to your business, without inviting a major investigation, which is likely to cost you a lot of money. Nonetheless, sensible expenses should always be attributed to the business, where possible.

Income tax and the self-employed

In Chapter 8 of this book, we will consider, in detail, the various ways in which you can trade. Undoubtedly, the simplest form of trading is to operate as a sole trader and as a self-employed person you will be taxed under what is known as Schedule D. This means you pay income tax in arrears at the end of each tax year, based on your income less all genuine business expenses. You can opt to be self-employed even if you work only for one customer, provided that you can convince the tax man as to the nature of your relationship – in other words, if your relationship is a contractual one, in which you are supplying either goods or services but your customer has no direct control over your time, then probably you will be entitled to self-employment status. The moment you set up in business, you must notify your local Inspector of Taxes, on form 41G. Thereafter, you are required to submit annual accounts showing details of your trading profit. The profit you make during the first 12 months of trading will be used as the basis for your tax assessment for each of the first three years. For this reason, it is actually attractive, from the point of view of tax, to keep your first year's profits as low as possible. Of course, you may need to demonstrate to backers and bankers that your business is viable by producing good profits and, unfortunately, there is always this conflict. Do bear in mind that the responsibility is yours to notify the Inland Revenue of your self-employment status and, bearing in mind that in your first year of trading you are quite likely to make a loss, it is particularly important for you to do so since you are likely to be entitled to a tax rebate. The reason for this is that the tax legislation is very kind to the newly self-employed person. If a loss is incurred in the first year of a new business, it can be offset against your income – not only in the year of loss but in the three years preceding the year in which you made the loss. This means that if you were employed during this period and then gave up employment to start your own business, opening losses will most probably entitle you to a tax rebate.

It would be wrong to talk about self-employment without touching again on that most controversial of subjects – *allowable expenses*. Here is a brief check-list of allowable expenses:

- rent and rates of business premises
- heat and light
- telephone
- motor expenses
- travelling, hotels, meals (but not entertaining)
- interest on loans
- professional charges
- insurance
- repairs and maintenance
- wages and salaries of employees.

Items of capital expenditure, such as equipment and machinery, are ultimately allowable against your pre-tax profits but you cannot claim 100 per cent of the cost in the year in which you bought the item. Capital allowances are a complicated business and it would be sensible to talk to an accountant if you are going to incur a lot of capital expenditure.

Do be sensible and businesslike about your business expenses and always try to make sure you can demonstrate to the tax man that you are not trying to take advantage of his questionable good nature!

National Insurance

This is a tax on the employer as well as the employee, which is something you need to bear in mind if you are considering employing someone. Similarly, if you are intending to form a company from which to operate your business, you yourself will have to pay National Insurance as an employee of the company, as well as the company paying on your behalf as the employer. If you are self-employed you still have to pay National Insurance. If you are employed and also run your own business, there are two lumps of National Insurance to be paid, linked to both your salary from your employed job and your earnings from your business. In other words, they have got you all ways round –

whatever your source of earnings, you are liable to pay a National Insurance contribution.

The sliding scale of charges (1988–89) payable by employee and employer are:

Wages (per week)	% rate payable on all earnings Employee	% rate payable on all earnings Employer
Up to £41.00	Nil	Nil
£41.00 – £69.99	5	5
£70.00 – £104.99	7	7
£105.00 – £154.99	9	9
£155.00 – £305.00	9	10.45
Additional charge over £305.00	Nil	10.45

Let us look at the various mixes of employment that might apply to you and see how these affect your National Insurance contribution.

National Insurance and the self-employed

The self-employed person pays what is called a Class 2 contribution, normally by way of stamps, which is currently £4.05 per week. However, there is a small earnings exemption which means that you do not have to pay Class 2 if your earnings from self-employment are expected to be less than £2,250 per annum. To qualify for a small earnings exemption you must apply to the DHSS *in advance*.

As a self-employed person you are also liable for Class 4 contributions, which are earnings related. You have to pay 6.3 per cent on profits or gains between £4,750 and £15,860 a year.

National Insurance for maintaining your job and being self-employed

If you are keeping your job going while starting a business, payment of Classes 2 and 4 can be deferred until after the end of the tax year. This is to avoid you making an overpayment, since your employed status will count towards your National Insurance contributions as a whole.

You have nothing to lose by being completely open with the DHSS and asking their advice on any National Insurance queries you may have. If you try and evade them, they will catch up with you in the end. By contrast, explaining your various problems to them could result in your actually being saved from making unnecessary contributions.

You are required to inform the DHSS before you start trading as a self-employed person and, contrary to how you might imagine them to be, you will find that they are very helpful people who will do their best to advise you about your new-found status. Take, for example, the exemption on self-employment I mentioned just now. Remember that we are not looking at total income but at income less expenses. You may well find that in your first year of trading, you can be confident that you will earn less than £2,250 – in which case you will be issued with an exemption notice that will mean you do not need to pay Class 2 contributions. If your earnings are going to be less than £800 a year, the DHSS do not even consider it necessary to issue you with an exemption notice, but nonetheless you must inform them of what you are doing – in the long term it saves a lot of hassle.

At the other end of the scale, if you are employed and earning £305 per week or more and are starting your own business on the side, any self-employed earnings you make will not be subject to deduction of National Insurance because you are already making an adequate contribution via your job.

It is important, therefore, not to view the DHSS as the enemy but to seek their advice to ensure that you pay no less, but equally well no more, than you need to.

Social security benefits

If you are seeking to start your own money-making venture, it may well be because you have been finding it difficult to obtain a job. If this is the case, you may have been relying heavily on social security benefits. It is very important to understand what happens to these benefits in the event of your starting your own business. Let us look at benefits in detail.

Unemployment benefit

The theory behind the qualification for unemployment benefit is that you are entitled to receive it *if you are immediately available for work* in the event of work being found for you. In the early days of starting a business, if you are working part-time from home and are prepared to drop everything and take any job offered to you, you may well be entitled to continue drawing unemployment benefit until such time as the business you are starting actually begins to bear fruit. I am not trying to mislead you or get you to purloin State funds but do not automatically assume that the day you open the doors for business is the day you have to stop drawing unemployment benefit. It probably would be sensible to discuss your position with your local DHSS office if you have doubts.

Supplementary benefits

- **supplementary allowances**
  What applies to unemployment benefit applies in general terms to supplementary allowances. If your pending business affects your benefit then, by inference, it will also affect your supplementary allowances. Check your position carefully with the DHSS office if you have any doubts.

- **supplementary pensions**
  We will look in detail at pensions next, but so far as supplementary pensions are concerned, if your business affects your basic State pension then obviously it will affect your supplementary pension. It is important to recognize with Supplementary pensions that your entitlement is based on need and you may well be able to demonstrate that the need remains, even though you are in the early stages of starting a business.

Pensions

- **occupational pension**
  An occupational pension is another way of describing a private pension, that is, a pension other than a state pension. Whatever the size of your occupational pension, it is in no way affected by any subsequent earnings you make.

- **state pension**
  You can earn up to £75 per week in additional income without it in any way affecting your pension. Thereafter you will suffer a 5 pence reduction in pension for every 10 pence earned between £75 and £79 per week. At over £79 per week, your pension is reduced on a one for one basis.

Family credit

As from April 1988 assistance is given to families on low incomes by means of a new family credit scheme, which replaces the previous family income supplement.

Family credit provides extra money for people who are working. It is payable to both men and women – couples or single parents. To qualify, you must be working for at least 24 hours a week and have at least one child under 16 (or between 16 and 18 and in full-time education). The level of benefit depends upon the amount you are earning and the number of children in the family. Being self-employed makes no difference to your entitlement to family credit – net profit from your business is taken into account instead of salary or wages.

The DHSS leaflet which introduced family credit does not quote a table of benefits, but gives an example of a family with three young children. The gross family income is quoted as £100 per week – assumed to be about £86.50 after tax and NI. This gives family credit of about £31 per week. This would be paid by an order book to be cashed each week at a post office, or by monthly credit transfer to your bank or building society account.

The leaflet explains that even if earnings are lower than the unemployment benefit which you would have got if you were not working, the total of your earnings and family credit will make you better off than being unemployed. So the scheme does act as a stimulus to get work or start your own business.

Redundancy payments

Redundancy payments are unaffected by any subsequent earnings, whether you are employed or self-employed.

Child benefit

However much you earn, you are still entitled to child benefit at the standard rate.

Student grants

If you have qualified for a student grant, you can earn £460 per year without it affecting the status of your grant. Earnings over £460 will restrict the amount of grant payable but not necessarily on a pound for pound basis. It depends on your circumstances and you should check out the position with your local authority.

Disability allowance

Invalidity pensions and allowances are paid because it is assumed that you cannot work because of the state of your health. If your health improves sufficiently so that you can start your own money-making venture, then, in virtually all cases, the money you earn will be deducted from your allowances. In a very few instances, the type of work you do could be considered remedial and in this case your allowances would not be affected. However, it has to be said that, whilst each case is judged on merit, it is very difficult to prove a case for remedial work that is also lucrative.

Maternity allowance

If you form your own company and are therefore employed by it, you are entitled to statutory maternity pay in the same was as you would be working for any other employer. This is payable for a maximum of 18 weeks, starting at the earliest in the eleventh week before the expected week of confinement, and at the latest, in the sixth week before the expected week of confinement. To qualify for SMP, you must have worked continuously for at least 26 weeks and into the fifteenth week before the expected week of confinement. This fifteenth week is known as *the qualifying week*. There are two rates of SMP payable – the higher rate, which is equal to 90 per cent of average earnings, is payable for the first six weeks and a lower fixed scale rate is payable for the balance of the 18-week entitlement. To qualify for the higher rate you have to have worked continuously for the same employer for at least two years, up to and including the qualifying week, and you must work at least 16 hours per week. Alternatively, you can have worked continuously for five years for the same employer at between 8 and 16 hours per week.

If you are self-employed or, indeed, not employed at all, you are entitled to a National Insurance maternity allowance of £31.30 per week for the whole of the 18-week period.

Statutory sick pay

If you are employed by your own company then you are entitled to up to 28 weeks of statutory sick pay in any one year but, as the employer, you can reclaim the SSP paid by deducting it from the PAYE and National Insurance liabilities each month. The current rates of SSP are:

- employees earning £79.50 or more, weekly, £49.20 per week
- employees earning £41 to £79.49, weekly, £34.25 per week

SSP is payable to all employees with the following exceptions:

- employees on short-term contract
- employees on strike
- employees earning less than £41 per week
- employees over retirement age

SSP is treated as earnings and is subject to the normal PAYE and National Insurance contributions.

If you are self-employed or for any other reason not entitled to SSP, National Insurance sickness benefit is payable at the rates indicated in the box.

Status	Benefit (per week)
single person	£31.30
single woman over 60	£39.45
married woman	£19.40
married woman over 60	£23.65

It is a minefield, the benefit business, and it is no good pretending otherwise. Once again though, I would stress it is important that you discuss your particular problems with the DHSS who really are there to help.

Corporation tax

If you are not intending to operate your business through a limited company then corporation tax does not apply to you – it is only payable by limited companies.

To help the smaller company, a two-tier rate of corporation tax has been introduced for companies whose profits are less than £100,000 per annum. For 1989, this rate is 25 per cent. Profits of over £500,000 are charged at the full rate of 35 per cent. There is marginal relief between £100,000 and £500,000. As with any form of taxation on the business, it is important here to emphasize the word *profit*. Corporation tax is payable on a company's profit, not turnover. For this reason, an important point to bear in mind is that as the principal in a company, it may be better from a tax point of view to draw a high salary and take no dividends than the reverse. The reason for this is that salaries are an allowable expense against corporation tax, whereas dividends paid to shareholders are paid out of taxed profits. I use the words 'may be better' advisedly, because it is a delicate balancing act to organize the most tax-effective relationship between profit, remunerations and dividend within a private company. If you draw extra salary in order to reduce corporation tax, you may start paying a higher rate of income tax – and the company will have to pay 10.45 per cent National Insurance on the extra salary. If, on the other hand, you leave the profit in the company, because corporation tax is 'only 25 per cent', how do you pay for your summer holiday? Drawing a dividend can be effective because although it will be taxed as income in your hands, it does not give rise to the extra National Insurance cost in the company.

Normally, corporation tax is payable nine months from the end of each accounting period but, depending on how long it takes you to finalize your accounts, there is a degree of leeway.

Value added tax (VAT)

At the time of starting your business, one of the decisions you have to make is whether you are going to register for VAT. If your sales are going to exceed the VAT threshold, which is currently £22,100 per annum, then you need to register with Customs and Excise as a taxable trader for VAT purposes. In some instances people register for VAT although they know their sales will not exceed this figure in the first year of trading and this you are entitled to do.

There are various reasons why you might be attracted to registering for VAT even if you do not have to. It might be that you are going to be investing a great deal of money in plant and equipment, in which case you can reclaim the VAT element on these purchases if you are registered. Alternatively, you might have the type of business where the materials you purchase are subject to VAT, but your sales are not. An example of this is children's clothes. You will have to pay VAT on fabric but VAT is not chargeable on the finished garment. In this instance it means that if you are not registered for VAT you have no means of reclaiming the VAT you have been charged on the fabric.

VAT works like this: you will pay VAT on virtually all your purchases and expenses. If you are registered for VAT then you will charge VAT on your sales unless you are dealing in an exempted or zero rated item. The difference between what you have charged on sales (VAT collected on behalf of the Government) and what you have paid on purchases is then accountable. If you have paid more than you have charged, which very often happens in the early days of business, then Customs and Excise will send you a cheque. If you have charged more than you have paid then you have to pay Customs and Excise. The completing of VAT returns is usually looked on by the small businessman as a tremendous hurdle but, in fact, if you have a proper system of record keeping, it should be no more than a 15 minute job. Your VAT return is only required to show totals – no details are presented at all – but from time to time, Customs and Excise may make routine checks on your documentation to see that you can support the returns you have put in.

Certain items are either exempt or zero rated for VAT purposes. Zero rated items include food and drink, children's clothing and protective clothing, books, newspapers and journals, medicines, equipment for the disabled, passenger transport, export and services to overseas traders, new buildings, caravans and house boats, gifts to charity, cultural and entertainment services. The difference between zero rating and exemption is that zero rated items are subject to VAT, it is just that the percentage of VAT charged is nought – a mad system, but this is the way it is expressed. Exempted items carry no VAT and these include the sale of land, insurance, postal services, financial services, health and education, professional bodies and trade unions, betting, gaming, burial and cremation.

By law, VAT returns have to be kept up to date and there are very strict fines and penalties for falling behind with payments. If you are suffering from a period of cash flow problems, make sure that you pay your VAT ahead of your other creditors for there are surcharges and penalties for late payment.

Capital Gains Tax (CGT)

I only mention Capital Gains Tax here because it may well be that you wish to give shares in your business to your family or you may be considering selling assets in order to raise capital for your business.

Capital gains are now taxable together with your income each year, so CGT is payable at 25 per cent or 40 per cent, depending on the combined level of income and capital gain. Taxable gains may arise on the disposal of all your assets, including gifts, except for quite specifically exempted items. The items that are exempt from CGT are as follows:

- transfers between husband and wife
- the disposal of your only or main residence
- sale of government stocks and certain corporate fixed interest stocks
- disposal arising from death
- personal belongings worth £3,000 or less at date of disposal or having a useful life of less than 50 years when you acquired them
- gifts to charity.

In addition to these exemptions, there is no CGT levied on the first £5,000 of capital gain in any one year but this exemption cannot be carried forward. This means that if you made no profit on any disposal of assets last year, you cannot employ the unused exemption this year. However, losses can be carried forward. If, say, you sold shares last year that raised £1,000 less than you paid for them, you can, at some time in the future, deduct that £1,000 of loss from any subsequent gain.

Watch CGT around the period of marriage. In the year of marriage, both husband and wife are entitled to their full £5,000 exemption and in that year of marriage only, if they both own a home they can each sell it and enjoy CGT exemption. Where CGT losses are brought forward, neither husband nor wife can offset those losses against each other's gains in the year of marriage, only against their own. Where a woman has CGT losses at the date of her marriage, they can be carried forward and set off against future gains made by either her or her husband. Finally, beware 6 April! If you marry on that date, which is the first day of the tax year, you will be treated as having been married for the whole of that fiscal year, so the above exemptions will not be available. If you must get married in early April, for heavens sake make it 7 April!

Again, it is worth stressing that, as with income tax, if you are separated or divorced, for Capital Gains Tax purposes you will be treated as a single person.

With the introduction of independent taxation, it is intended that, from 6 April 1990, a husband and wife will be treated as single persons for Capital Gains Tax.

The 1988 Finance Act has introduced a new basis for the calculation of capital gains, so that only gains arising from 1 April, 1982 will now be taxable. There are complex transitional arrangements to cover this change in the rules. If you are considering selling a major asset I would advise you to seek the advice of your solicitor or accountant before proceeding with it. It is a tricky business and professional advice will more than earn its keep.

Inheritance tax

I am only mentioning inheritance tax to ensure that you are aware of the implications of any estate you may have inherited. It is important that you do not commit yourself to using the money – perhaps on the starting of a new business – without being aware of the taxation implications.

No inheritance tax is charged on an estate where the total value transferred is less than £110,000 and in addition there are a number of exemptions that you should check out carefully with your solicitor. Relief from the full impact of inheritance tax at the 40 per cent flat rate is also given on both lifetime gifts and transfers of business assets and here again it is very important that you fully understand what this means. If you are either the beneficiary of an estate or have built up a valuable business that you wish to pass on to your children or colleague then, at the earliest possible opportunity, seek professional advice. Transferring an asset in the *right* way can greatly reduce the full impact of inheritance tax.

7 Business location

The location of your business can be absolutely fundamental to its success, or of no consequence at all. If you are intending to open a retail outlet, location has to be the major concern, whereas if you are a freelance journalist you can probably work anywhere. Let us look at the various options open to you.

Working from home

For any new business starting with limited capital, working from home has to be a very attractive proposition as clearly there will be enormous cost advantages. The savings involved not only include the more obvious overheads of rent, rates, heat and light but there are also savings to be made on travelling to work, lunches, installation of a telephone line and, of course, perhaps the most important saving of all – time. Whilst working at home is attractive to any first-time businessman, to women, clearly, it has particular relevance. If you have children, working away from home implies the additional cost of a mother's help or the generally unsatisfactory business of having to farm out your children with friends. One of the main reasons you may be considering starting your own venture is because you want to combine family life with commercial considerations and, certainly, working from home will make this a great deal easier.

Before we consider the legislation involved in working from home, let us just look at the everyday practicalities. Whatever your occupation, if humanly possible, do run your business from a room that can be allocated to you and you alone. If you are trying to work on the kitchen table (yes, I know Laura Ashley started her business there!), the fact is that you will be endlessly interrupted, you will be disruptive to family life and every time you want to have a meal, your business will have to be packed away. The little business you started out feeling so enthusiastic about will soon become a major aggravation factor within the family.

Trying to work in the hub of

family life is also a bad discipline, both for you and your family. If you have a room of your own, you can inform your family that they may enter it in a dire emergency but otherwise they must leave you alone. In other words, they have the comfort of knowing you are about and you have the comfort of knowing that they will come screaming if anything goes wrong. It means everyone can get on with their pursuits without treading on each other's toes.

A personal case history *A few weeks ago, I found that my little office off the kitchen was just no longer conducive to concentrated bouts of writing, mainly because of an increasing number of children and* *animals about the place. I persuaded my husband to build me a hut at the bottom of the garden and when it was completed, I held a hut warming party for the whole family. We did it properly – champagne, the lot – and all members of the family were allowed to inspect my hut – not a long job, it is only 6 by 9 feet! The inspection completed, I announced to them all that they would never see the inside of my hut again, that when I was in it, I was never to be disturbed and that if anyone telephoned, they were to be told I was out. The result – it works, it's glorious... I have uninterrupted peace in the bosom of my family!*

I really do strongly advise you to try and achieve the same sort of arrangement. If you have a spare room, use that. Seriously, how often do you have people to stay? Get rid of the bedroom furniture, use the money to buy a sofa bed to put in your living room and turn the spare room into a full-time workroom. If the family do not like it, tell them that once you have made your fortune you will build them an extension – that should keep them quiet. If you have no available spare room, why not operate from a garden shed like I do. A shed need cost no more than a couple of hundred pounds. Line it with some insulating board, buy a heater and you are all set up – oh, and do not forget the thermos of coffee!

Being on your own gives you time to concentrate and plan and allows you to have disciplined hours of work. I 'commute' to work at nine o'clock every morning, come 'home' for lunch and then work again in the afternoon until school finishes. If I tried to achieve the same thing in the kitchen, I would find all sorts of excuses not to work – the hob looks dirty, the dog needs walking – the list is endless. You have to put these domestic considerations behind you in just the same way as anyone who goes out to work must do.

Let us now look at the legal implications of working from home. There are both internal and external forces at work that may make it difficult for you to operate certain types of business from your home. The internal forces are certain contractual relationships into which you may have already entered, without perhaps being aware of them. If you rent your house it could well be that in the lease you are quite specifically prohibited from conducting any kind of commercial enterprise on the premises. If you own your own house, it may be that, at the time of purchase, you accepted a covenant that, again, prohibits commercial use. If you are a home owner or a tenant, you may have entered into some sort of agreement with the tenants' association or neighbourhood association geared towards the protection of the environment, which also prohibits commercial use. Sometimes mortgage agreements carry a proviso that no business may be carried on in the premises. If you feel you may have entered into any one of these contractual relationships, I would suggest that first you talk the matter through with your solicitor. So much depends on what you are actually planning to do. It may well be that your solicitor feels it is reasonable for you to go ahead with your plans because of the nature of your occupation. Alternatively, it may be possible for you to renegotiate the terms of lease, mortgage, covenant or other contract. Whatever the circumstances, it is important that you are aware that these sort of restrictions could be already imposed upon you.

The external forces that are likely to impose restrictions upon you are essentially local authorities – more particularly planning, highways and health and safety. I have talked long and exhaustively to the planning authorities about working from home. It is a fact that, legally, if you have a desk, a typewriter, a filing cabinet and a telephone in an area designated for work, then technically you need planning permission, for it implies *a material change of use* from the domestic purposes for which your home was intended. However, if everyone who worked from home applied to their local planning authority for permission to do so, the authorities are the first to admit that they would be absolutely appalled and quite unable to cope.

It is a question of interpreting what is meant by *material change of use*, and probably the best yardstick to use is the likely attitudes of your neighbours. If you are intending to start a theatre ticket booking agency from home, which involves virtually no callers, since all your business takes place on the telephone, then such a business is not going to affect the environment in any way. If you are going into the antique restoration business and, three or four times a week, a large pantechnicon is parked outside your house for a couple of hours, and the rest of the week the neighbourhood rings with the sounds of your hammering – then this certainly qualifies as *material change of use*.

When all is said and done, the planning restrictions are really based on a question of good neighbourliness. If you are carrying on a quiet unobtrusive business, then the planning authorities will turn a blind eye. If they receive a complaint from a neighbour about your activities, they are obliged to follow up that complaint and may ultimately force you to close down. It is all about common sense and so much depends upon your environment as to how you interpret the planning implications. If you live in a bedsit, with paper-thin walls, then almost anything you do is going to be disruptive and cause trouble. If you live in a cottage on the side of a mountain, five miles from the nearest house, you can do almost anything you like! Try and look at your activities from your neighbours' point of view – you may be so absorbed in giving piano lessons, that you do not consider how incredibly irritating it is for your neighbours to hear the same tune repeated again and again, with varying degrees of accuracy. The cost of sound-proofing a practice room pales into insignificance compared with restrictions that could be placed upon you as to when you can and cannot take pupils or, indeed, whether you can take them at all.

A couple of dire warnings to consider:

- **Insurance** No ordinary householders' insurance policy covers for commercial accidents. If your enamelling kiln blows up in your face and burns the house down and your insurance company finds out that you were operating an enamelling business they knew nothing about, they could refuse to accept any liability and you could find yourself homeless. It is an extreme example, but it *could* happen. If you are undertaking any sort of commercial enterprise that could involve a risk (and that is almost everything) then talk to an insurance broker and get the necessary cover.
- **Capital Gains Tax implications** We dealt in brief in the last chapter with Capital Gains Tax and, as you will be aware, if you come to sell your main or only dwelling house, you do not have to pay Capital Gains Tax on it. With the current escalation in property prices, this has to be the best possible way of increasing your capital base these days and trading up, in terms of house purchase, is the way many people make provision for their old age. However, if a portion of your house is quite clearly designated as commercial premises at the time of sale, then you will have to pay capital gains tax on *that portion* of your home. For this reason, it is simply not worth creating any formal relationship between your business and your home. In other words, if 25 per cent of your home is being used for your business, you could legitimately charge your

business a rent and, in addition, pay a proportion of the rates, light and heat through the business, but *do not do it*, and if you have any doubts about how far you can go without falling into the CGT trap, do consult an accountant.

Supplying food to the public

Under the heading of working from home, I think it particularly important to mention the preparation of food for it is, potentially, a very fraught area. There are very stringent rules and regulations appertaining to the supply of food to the public and you should not attempt to take any short cuts when it comes to following these regulations. Firstly, you need to purchase from HMSO a copy of *Your Guide to Food Hygiene (General Regulations), 1970*. This leaflet can also be obtained from the Health

Education Council, 78 New Oxford Street, London WC1A 1AH, and is very helpful in outlining the rules and regulations – if a little daunting. If you are going in for any form of catering, obviously the major consideration is your kitchen. Your kitchen must not lead into a bedroom, toilet or bathroom. It must be scrupulously clean, no rubbish should be lying around and well-maintained – no cracked work surfaces or crumbling plaster. There must be two sinks, one for washing hands and the other to be used for usual kitchen purposes. There must be two refrigerators – one for cooked meat and one for uncooked meat and a number of chopping boards so that meat and vegetables are never chopped on the same board. Stainless steel is favoured for working surfaces and sinks. Animals must be completely banned. When working you should wear protective clothing and have some covering for your head. There is also a requirement to have a first-aid kit to hand.

If the business you are intending to run is small, provided you put these regulations into effect, there is no need to draw the Environmental Health officer's attention to what you are doing. If, however, you are investing a considerable amount of capital in, say, a restaurant or café then, before you open the doors to the public, it
is sensible to invite along the Environmental Health officer and ask his advice as to what needs to be done to the premises. Indeed, I would go so far as to suggest that you should involve him before you even commit yourself to buying or leasing the premises for, in some cases, the amount of work needed on a kitchen could cost thousands of pounds. Again, common sense should prevail. A high standard of hygiene is essential to ensure that the goods you produce will do no one any harm. A complaint of food poisoning can have you closed down overnight.

Note also that the legislation regarding food hygiene covers the transport of food as well. There is a leaflet called *The Food Hygiene (Market Stalls and Delivery Vehicles) Regulations, 1966,* which is available from the Health Education Council. You should study this if you are intending to become involved in any form of outside catering.

In conclusion, therefore, in order to work trouble-free from home, if you upset no one then no one will interfere with you. It is basically as simple as that.

Renting a property

If your business requires its own premises then, as a general rule, you would be advised to rent rather than make an outright purchase. Obviously a purchase will involve you in a great deal of capital and there are far more leasehold premises available that are likely to be suitable for your needs. Small freehold properties are very rarely built for commercial use – they have to be converted, which is often both expensive and not particularly satisfactory in the end.

Let us now look at three types of leasehold property.

Acquiring a new lease

Most landlords with industrial premises are finding it quite difficult to obtain suitable tenants these days. This applies particularly where developers have built new commercial units and are trying to sell the leases of the premises for the first time. This factor is very important to remember. When you are approached by a landlord with a new lease on offer, he will present you with a draft lease setting out the terms for renting the premises. When you start querying some of those terms, he will say that they are not open to negotiation because these are his standard terms. This is frequently absolute rubbish and simply an old chestnut that landlords will hand you. If you are in the business of acquiring a new lease, then that lease should be entered into on *your* terms not on the landlord's. If your demands are reasonable and the landlord will not bend, then do not take the lease – it is as simple as that.

You should not enter into a commercial lease of any sort without consulting a solicitor, but here are a few pointers to use as a check-list when looking at the terms of a new lease:

- check the user clause in the lease and make sure that whatever your business occupation, it will be covered by that user clause

- check with the Planning Department of your local Authority that the landlord has built the premises to their satisfaction and that he has permission to use the premises for commercial purposes – and, indeed, make sure that he has title to the premises. Do not simply accept the landlord's word for all this

- compare the rent you are being asked to pay with other rentals in the area. If it is high, do not accept it

- with new premises you are bound to want extra fixtures and fittings, and, in consideration of these, your landlord may well ask for an increased rent. Make sure this is negotiated before he begins work, and the additional rent is reasonable

- on modern industrial estates, access, parking and loading areas around the buildings are very often poorly defined. You need to know how many car parking spaces you have been allocated, exactly where they are, and whether in practice the number of parking spaces is feasible in terms of turning area and other requirements. You also need to have a very clear understanding of the position with regard to loading and unloading.

- most landlords will require a personal guarantee against the rent, particularly if you are setting up a new business as a limited company. Still more insulting, some will actually ask for a personal guarantee from your *husband!* You may have to swallow your pride on this one in order to obtain the premises but never sign an open-ended guarantee. Link the guarantee to a period of, say, three or four years, or to an agreed profit figure

- clarify the position with regard to assigning the lease or sub-letting part of the premises. You do not know what is going to happen to your business in the next few years but it may well be that you out-grow the premises quite quickly or that you, in fact, do not need as much space as you had anticipated. Try and build, into whatever lease you take, as much flexibility as possible

- landlords normally like to arrange the insurance themselves and then look to you to pay for it. Make sure you are not being over-charged, and make sure you know exactly what cover is being provided and therefore what risks are still outstanding, and for which you need to cover yourself

- Look very carefully at repair and reinstatement commitments. Normally a lease demands that the property is returned to the landlord in exactly the same state as it was when you acquired the lease. This clause can prove expensive in two ways. If in fact the building is in need of constant repair, you could find that over the years you have to spend an absolute fortune on it in order to maintain it at the standard it was when you acquired the lease. The other trap you can fall into is with regard to what you consider to be improvements – building an extra office, putting in an additional floor, etc., etc. The landlord may argue at the time of surrendering the lease, that conversions of this sort were for your benefit not his so whilst he may have given you permission to do it, he may demand that these so-called improvements are taken down before you leave the premises.

Taking over an existing lease

When you take over the lease of existing premises you, of course, cannot vary the terms. In addition, you may be asked to pay a premium to the departing tenant in order to acquire his or her lease. There are various reasons why you might be asked to pay a premium. High premiums are often paid to reflect the value of goodwill, because a business has been established on the premises. For example, take a restaurant. The departing tenant may have acquired a licence, built up a clientele and extensively converted the property to make it suitable for a restaurant. In these circumstances, he will be looking for some kind of recompense for what he has put into the premises.

A premium may also be asked if the terms of the lease are particularly attractive – in other words, the scale of rentals has not kept pace with inflation, there is a long time before the next rent review and, therefore, future rentals will be low. Premiums may also be charged if the departing tenant has extensively altered and improved the premises and if he is intending to leave behind a number of fixtures and fittings.

In many cases, the charging of a premium may be justified, but you do have to be cautious. If you are taking over the lease of a restaurant that you are intending to change into a cocktail bar, then much of the goodwill element being charged by way of premium is simply not relevant to you. The departing tenant's fixtures and improvements may have made *his* life a lot easier but are they what *you* want? If they are not, then they are worthless. A note of caution here: as mentioned under new leases, do watch the reinstatement clauses for you might find yourself responsible for reinstating the former tenant's conversions. Another aspect of this, of course, is to be careful about maintenance. Before taking over a lease, you should check very carefully the maintenance obligations. If necessary have a survey done for you, and make sure that you are not committing yourself to major expenditure during, or at the end, of the lease. If you have to hand the property back at the end of the lease in first class order, but the roof already needs renewing, that is an obligation you have to sort out with the existing tenant now. It is no good trying to argue with the landlord after you have taken on the lease.

Sometimes it is well worth acquiring a lease with just a short period to run on it. Particularly if you have a new business and you are uncertain as to how it is going to grow, small premises with a commitment of, say, just 18 months left on the lease could be very attractive and it is unlikely that there will be much of a premium, if any. In these circumstances, if the premises prove right for you, you are entitled, under The Landlord and Tenant Act, to an automatic right to renewal at an open market rent. For peace of mind though, if you can negotiate the new lease before committing yourself to the old, at least you will know the future position should you wish to take it up.

Lastly, it is always important to try and establish why the existing tenant is leaving the premises, particularly if the premises are going to play a vital role in the success or failure of your business – for instance in the case of a shop or restaurant. Ask around the neighbourhood and make sure you know everything there is to know before committing yourself.

Subsidized premises

If you are looking for a leasehold property, it is well worth contacting your local authority to see if there are any subsidized premises available in your area. There are grants available, subsidized rentals and rent-free periods all going begging in development areas. Many local authorities have developed what they call *nursery units*, aimed quite specifically at the new business where small premises at low rentals are available. You can write to the Department of Trade and Industry, 1–19 Victoria Street, London SW1H 0ET, who will give you details of subsidized premises and locations.

Buying a property

It always amazes me how little time people seem to spend on what has to be the major purchase of their life – their own home. If you have ever sold a house, I am sure you will have been aware of how people look around just once or twice, spend half an hour whispering in corners and then, incredibly, make you an offer! They would take a great deal more time over choosing a new car or even a new washing machine, but such is the system of house buying in this country, it is so pressurized and fraught that there seems to be no time for careful consideration.

If you are intending to buy a freehold property for industrial purposes, you have to take time and not throw caution to the wind. There are so many considerations – planning permission, of course, is the major one but, whilst you might have obtained change of use, there are still the problems of fire regulations and health and safety. There are also the questions of access, parking, whether the floors have sufficient load-bearing capacity for the machinery you intend using and so on. No one is going to tell you any of these things, you have to think out every eventuality yourself and all too often serious mistakes are made. Available from HMSO is a booklet called *Planning Permission a Guide to Industry*, which you will find helpful. It would also be worthwhile contacting the Department of Industry, Millbank Tower, Millbank, London SW1P 4QU (telephone: 01-211 6486), who will be able to give you a list of existing industrial freehold premises available, often for expansion and development.

One way in which the buying of a freehold property for business purposes can be justified is when you are linking home and business. If you are intending to run a shop, a restaurant or a café, buying the whole building and living above the business could make both the running and the profitability of your business a great deal easier. If you would like to run a bed and breakfast business and your existing home is not suitable, then a move to a larger house could be the answer. Again, though, watch the CGT implications and make sure that the least possible amount of space is allocated to the business – in official terms, at any rate!

As with any freehold purchase, a survey and searches are part of the standard procedure, but your searches should be particularly thorough. Supposing the fastest access to your premises is down a road lined with residential houses and you know you will be having lorries coming in and out, all hours of the day and night. The amount of hassle you are likely to receive in these circumstances may actually make the purchase of that particular freehold nonviable. Brick build your security so that you are absolutely confident you can carry on the work you want to do on the premises, not only now, but in the future when the nature of your business – by virtue of expansion – may change or develop. Never, in my view, should you purchase premises without having first acquired permission for commercial use unless you have unlimited time and money to burn.

This then completes the look at business premises. Do take time and trouble to assess your requirements and do not rush into anything. Remember that in the early days of a business, its location requirements can change enormously, so be cautious of making commitments that cannot be altered or renegotiated.

8 Business structure

Having selected the type of business venture you intend running, the natural progression is to decide in what form it is going to be run. The three main ways of trading are as *a sole trader, a partnership* or as *a limited company*. Additionally you might consider buying an existing business or taking out a franchise because, in either case, you would eliminate some of the trauma of starting from scratch. Let us look at these different trading situations.

Sole trading

It is the most popular, the simplest and the cheapest method of going into business and, in many instances, it is also the best. You can start *right now* as a sole trader. You can call your business more or less what you like and open the doors for custom before the day is out. It really is as simple as that, and for those of you who cannot bear paperwork and red tape, as a sole trader you will attract the very minimum. Having said that, there are various disciplines that either you should inflict on yourself or that will be inflicted upon you. Let us look at self-inflicted disciplines first.

The most important self-discipline as a sole trader is to ensure that all your business transactions in a financial sense are kept entirely separate from your personal finances. If your business really is on an extremely small scale, this could involve nothing more than two purses. I have a friend living in Vancouver Island who runs a smallholding. The extent of her separate financing is that she has 'an egg purse' and 'an udder purse', which are fairly self-explanatory. All the money she obtains from selling eggs and milk go into the appropriate purses and she buys the chicken and cattle feed from them respectively. Every now and again she pockets the build up of surplus cash! Simple yes, but effective.

Assuming, however, that your business is going to be a little more ambitious than this, the first thing you need to do is to open a separate bank account. Into this account you should pay any capital you are investing or which is being invested in the business and, thereafter, you should pay all monies received into this account and write only business cheques from it. As a sole trader, it is very tempting to treat your business simply as an extension of yourself. However, if you do this you will find yourself in an appalling muddle and never know whether you are making a profit or not. In Chapter 10, we will be looking in detail at book-keeping and administrative systems – suffice to say here that, as a sole trader, you must not fail to recognize the separate identity of your business.

The disciplines required of a sole trader, by law, are very simple:

- you must always keep an up-to-date set of books and records for tax purposes, because the tax authorities may want to inspect these and, in any event, you will need them in order to complete your tax returns under schedule D

- if you are intending to employ anybody then you will need to make PAYE returns and be aware of the rules and regulations in connection with hiring and firing staff. In this respect you will find that your local DHSS department and tax office will be very helpful in setting you up with the necessary paperwork and ensuring you understand how it works

- you will have to register for VAT if you anticipate that your sales will exceed the VAT threshold (currently £22,100). If this is the case, you must notify your local Customs and Excise Department *before* you start trading and, of course, once registered, you will be committed to making VAT returns. If you start trading and your sales reach £7,500 in any calendar quarter, you must notify the VAT Office. You will be registered for VAT unless you still believe your annual sales will be below the £22,100 limit.

There are – as with everything – advantages and disadvantages in being a sole trader. You may well experience a degree of loneliness and isolation and feel intimidated by having total responsibility for what happens within your business – and then, of course, there are the financial implications. Protected by a limited company or sharing responsibilities with a partner or partners, if things go wrong, you have a degree of protection against the burden of debt and possible bankruptcy – not so the sole trader. If you get yourself into a mess, then only you can bale yourself out and if you cannot pay your business debts you may have to sell your house and all your possessions in order to satisfy your creditors. Of course, the reverse of this is that whilst you are wholly responsible if things go wrong, you are also wholly responsible if things go right – there is no one else with whom you have to share the profits – they are all yours and so is the glory of achievement. Presumably, one of the reasons you are even contemplating a business of your own is because you want an element of freedom that you have not enjoyed as an employed person. Tied down by the demands of a partner or co-directors in a limited company, you may find you are no more independent than you were as an employee. As a sole trader, the heady joys of doing precisely what you want, are all yours.

I have already mentioned that women find it more difficult than most men to be taken seriously when it comes to starting their own business. This factor is worth considering when deciding on the merits of being a sole trader. It should not be the case but, for some reason, operating as an individual, as opposed to a limited company, does seem to impress everyone a very great deal less. When it comes to borrowing money, setting up credit terms with a supplier or persuading a landlord that you can afford to pay the rent, being a limited company does help. Of course being protected by a limited company does not make you any more respectable – if anything it makes you less so – but for some reason everyone seems to prefer it. Probably, the implication is that they assume a limited company means you are seriously in business and not playing at it and since a woman often has this problem anyway, maybe a limited company is a better vehicle to use for serious trading.

I should mention, however, that there is no restriction on the size of a sole trader's business – in fact there are some very sizeable businesses around that are operated in this way. Remember there is no reason at all why you should commit yourself to becoming involved with other people, if you prefer to work alone.

Partnerships

Partnerships can be wonderful, they also can be appalling, and whether they succeed or not depends almost entirely on the way that they are set up in the first place. As we discussed when considering finance, one of the reasons you might want a partner is because you have the business idea and the skill to operate it, but you have no cash. There is nothing wrong with a partnership based on this type of arrangement because, in these circumstances, both you and your partner are contributing entirely different elements to the business and this really is the crux of a successful partnership.

Let us assume you have a friend who perhaps you met at playgroup when your children were both tiny and now, like you, has time on her hands because her children are at school full-time. Neither of you fancy the idea of going back to employment and, in any case, there are not many opportunities in your area. So, you decide to start a business together – a partnership. In theory there is nothing wrong with this, for what you have both recognized is mutual need and, since you are friends, you enjoy spending time together. However, this is absolutely no basis for a partnership. If you are going to become involved with a business partner, then the only criteria for taking on such a relationship is because he or she can provide you with something you cannot provide yourself – be it skill, money, premises, time, contacts, whatever. Only this way does the partnership stand a chance of working.

Let us now look at the structure of a partnership. There is no need for you to be equal partners and one of the most important elements of partnership is to establish the ratio of contribution to the business right from the very beginning, so that profits or earnings can be split on a pro rata basis. Having decided how the business should be carved up in terms of who is going to receive what, the next thing you need is a partnership agreement – a formal, written partnership agreement, signed by you both, and this applies whether your partner is your husband, your lover, your mother, your best friend, your brother, your daughter or your son. Things go wrong with relationships, even the best. Things also have a habit of going wrong with businesses. People fight more about money than they do about anything else and, right from the outset of your business you want to be absolutely clear as to how the partnership will be operated. Your solicitor will have a standard partnership agreement that may need amending. Having agreed the terms, having signed it and having filed it away, you will probably never need to refer to it again. However, should you be faced with a catastrophe – one of you dies or is taken seriously ill or the business gets into dire financial straits – then you can take out the agreement, dust it down and it will tell you what you both agreed to do in the circumstances.

If one of you is a great deal better off financially than the other, you could consider a limited partnership. In an ordinary partnership you are both responsible, equally, for the debts of the business and if one cannot pay his or her share then the other partner is responsible for his or her own share, plus what the other partner cannot pay. In a limited partnership, the partner with few resources can opt for limited liability to an agreed figure – in other words that partner only has to meet claims from creditors up to, shall we say, the sum of £2,500. If, therefore, the partnership is faced with a debt of £6,000, the partner with the limited liability only has to be responsible for £2,500 of that figure. Limited partnerships are sometimes useful where more than two partners are involved. It would be sensible to make the point here that partnerships are not necessarily between two people – you can have as many partners as you like, though one has to say the more partners you have, the more you will be increasing your headaches! If you are to form a limited partnership you do have to register it with the Registrar of Companies.

A personal case history *My daughter, Lucy, and I decided to go into business together breeding lovebirds, a short while ago. What prompted the whole venture was that we gave Lucy a pair of lovebirds last November and this spring they produced five healthy babies. The basis of our partnership is 50/50 – the idea being that we put in equal amounts of capital and draw* equally on our profits. The business has been operating now for all of five weeks. I have already invested over double Lucy's contribution. I do all the work, and she is still drawing 50 per cent of the profits. Lesson: I should practise what I preach!

One final point on partnerships: do remember that you are entirely responsible for each other's actions. That is no problem, you say, we are joint signatories on the bank account so there is no way my partner can get us into trouble without my knowing about it. Wrong. Your partner could go along tomorrow to your supplier and order £20,000 of goods on behalf of the partnership. These goods could be delivered and the partnership would be responsible for paying for them whether the money is available or not. Trust, therefore, is a very necessary ingredient, as is a sound, but in my view, not too close relationship. Close friendships tend to fudge the issue. Far better form a partnership with someone whose contribution you need and, as the partnership grows, so will the friendship. Forming a partnership with a great friend will lead inevitably to a very high expectation of your business relationship, which may not be justified. Good friends can be terribly tiresome workmates, and vice versa.

Limited companies

When you form a limited company you create an entirely separate legal entity. To form a company you generally need a minimum of two directors so, up to a point, you lose the feeling of your own personal business. However, your co-director could be a member of your family who has nothing to do with the day-to-day running of the business. In addition to two directors, you also need a company secretary, although very often your solicitor will handle this role for you. You can approach the registrar of companies yourself to form a limited company but it is far more sensible to deal through a solicitor, who will most probably buy a company 'off the shelf' for you. Buying a company 'off the shelf' means that you acquire a company that has been incorporated but has not yet traded and this is the cheapest and easiest way of forming a limited company. These dormant companies have extremely strange names so, in addition to the cost of purchase, you are likely to want to register a new name with the registrar of companies. The cost of getting this far might, typically, be about £300.

Once you have acquired the company, then you can issue shares. At the time of a company's formation, it has what is known as *authorized capital* which represents the amount of capital that is available for issue under its constitution. You have to decide how much permanent share capital you need to put into the company. If your business does not require any real capital base, issuing £100 of shares will be adequate. If you are going to be trading substantially, however, you will need to demonstrate the stability of the company to the bank, your suppliers and perhaps your customers. In these circumstances the *issued capital* might be £1,000 or even £10,000. If you are going into business with someone else, or a number of colleagues, the share capital you decide to subscribe will be issued between you in the proportions required to represent your respective 'stakes' in the business. Every company must have a minimum of two shareholders, so if the business is to be 100 per cent yours, with no one sharing the equity with you, there will need to be at least one share registered in another person's name on your behalf. This might be your husband, a friend or your solicitor and they will hold that share merely as your nominee. Once shareholders have taken up their shares and paid over their capital, the money invested is known as *paid-up capital*. Shareholders do not have to take up all the shares allocated to them at the time of formation, although it is normal to do so. Subject to considering taxation implications, existing shareholders, employees or outsiders may be granted options to purchase shares at a later date.

There are distinct advantages in running your business under the umbrella of a limited company. You will be taken more seriously in the business world and you will be protected personally from financial ruin if things go wrong, provided you have not committed yourself to personal guarantees. If you like, limited companies are people in their own right. They can be sued, they can own property and therefore the directors – except in the case of malpractice – are protected if things go wrong. A limited company also inflicts disciplines on its directors, which is no bad thing, since it is required to submit annual accounts to the registrar of companies. It should be mentioned that the preparation of these accounts will require an audit by a firm of accountants and an annual audit fee will add considerably to your overhead costs.

I have referred to the constitution of the company. On its formation, every company adopts a set of rules under which it has to operate. There are the Memorandum of Association (which specifies the name, the authorized capital and the main objects of the company) and the Articles of Association (which defines the detailed formalities for the company's operation – rights of shareholders, the way shares are dealt with, duties and relationship of directors, and so forth). Both the Memorandum and the Articles can be changed from time to time by the shareholders, but if you are buying a company off the shelf, your solicitor will aim to acquire one that has an existing Memorandum of Association applicable to your business. Certainly, the business types are fairly loosely defined, but it would be sensible in acquiring a company to think, not only of your requirements today, but of your likely requirements tomorrow. You may have a company whose Memorandum allows you to run a market garden but it could be that the herbs you are growing today, you may wish to mail order in a couple of years time. If this is the case, are you covered for so doing?

Buying an existing business

If a business is to fail, more often than not, it does so in the first few years of trading. An alternative to coping with all the teething troubles yourself is to buy an established business. Of course, in these circumstances one is immediately faced with the fact that a substantial sum of money may be required.

Alternatively you could buy a business that is actually losing money and therefore costs very little – if anything – provided you have enough confidence to believe that you can turn it into a profitable operation. If you are considering buying a business, however small, you must have professional help, in the form of an accountant, to thoroughly check the books and a solicitor to handle the legalities. In addition, I would suggest that you do not buy a business in a trade about which you know nothing. What may seem a good investment on the face of it, may prove the very opposite if you do not have experience of the trade. Certainly, if you are taking over a failing business you must know what you are doing and, whilst it is always tempting to assume one can do better than your predecessor, you need to be very clear as to why things have been going wrong, so that you can satisfy yourself that you can put things right.

A business will be comprised of assets and liabilities and, obviously, the person selling you the business will be making the most of the assets while playing down the liabilities. Remember that assets should be viewed as what they are worth to you. If you see that the way of progressing the business is to change its direction, then it could be that many of the assets are of no value at all – in which case you do not want them and should certainly pay very little for them. Stock is likely to be one of the most contentious issues. Chances are that the stock lying around will be dead stock or at any rate end-of-line. Carrying too much of the wrong stock is a killer for any business so be wary in paying the full value for it unless you can be absolutely sure of shifting it. Watch debtors, too. While the business allegedly may be owed a great deal of money by varying customers, make sure that these debts are not in dispute. Check the position of any property for sale and have someone with experience test the equipment.

When it comes to liabilities, it is very important that your accountant identifies all the liabilities owed by the vendor – all the trade debts, tax implications, pension commitments, mortgages and loans. If you are intending to make a number of redundancies, you need to calculate what sort of money will be involved in this, and your solicitor should see that there is no current litigation in process. Finally, when you believe you have established the true figures, you should not proceed with the purchase of the business unless the vendor will give you a warranty (in other words an undertaking) that the assets and liabilities are as stated. Always the cynic, I would just make the point that you should also satisfy yourself that the warranty the vendor has given you is worth something. Has he any personal resources to draw on if you have to sue him? If you have any doubts on that point, hold back part of the purchase price for long enough for you to get your feet under the table and thus make sure that any problem areas have been exposed.

Franchising

There is always a degree of funny media coverage on the subject of franchising. Franchise operations that have gone wrong are very often the subject of watch-dog investigations, which are usually more than amply justified. Yet at its best, franchising offers the would-be entrepreneur a safe and secure passage into the world of private enterprise.

What exactly is meant by the term *franchise*? It is this – a well-established company offers an individual the opportunity to trade under their corporate brand name. The company (known as the franchisor) offers the individual (known as the franchisee) a proven product and a wealth of commercial experience. The franchisee normally pays for the privilege by way of a one-off standard fee and thereafter a continuing royalty based on sales performance. The principle behind a franchise operation is that if a company has already established successful franchises in, say, London,

108

Reading, Bradford, Swansea and Glasgow, then there is no reason why they should not work anywhere else in the country. One of the most difficult aspects of starting your own business is finding a market, recognizing it when you do so and then being able to tap it for all you are worth. If you tie yourself in with a successful franchisor, the market is already proven and established and all you have to do is to sell to it. In many instances, the franchise operation provides you with the product, and with very detailed back-up of how to sell it. This is certainly true of many franchise restaurant operations and specialist shops such as The Body Shop.

From a woman's point of view, if you have been away from work for some years, raising children, you may feel that you are very much out of touch with the commercial world and, therefore, do not have the confidence to strike out on your own. If, instead, you buy a franchise you have someone working right alongside you and holding your hand. Not only is this very comforting, it will greatly enhance your chances of success. On the subject of success, figures quoted suggest that only between 1 – 2 per cent of franchises actually fail. This does give you a much higher chance of potential success than starting a business on your own.

It all sounds too good to be true, doesn't it? I must admit to having fairly lukewarm feelings towards many franchise operations. To start with, if you are risking your own money in a business, why should you risk it in someone else's business rather than your own. If you run a Prontaprint Shop or a Wimpy Bar or sort drains out under the name of Dynorod, you have none of the prestige of owning your own business. Talking to a Prontaprint franchisee not so long ago, she told me that everybody who wanted to see her always asked for the manager, not the proprietor, although of course the premises and the business are hers.

There is also the rather nebulous question of goodwill. If you set up a business today and run it profitably and successfully for the next ten years, you have something to hand over to your son or daughter, or something to sell to provide a handsome nest egg for the future. Not so with a franchise operation. Most franchise agreements only last for five years and, although they are renewable, you are not actually building anything. In some respects you could say that you are really no better off than being employed and yet you are having to risk your own capital.

Despite these gloomy thoughts, if you feel that you would like to go into business on your own but recognise that you will never have the confidence to do it, then it would be sensible to at least consider the franchise route. Be very careful, though, that you only become involved with recognized, well-established companies. The best way to safeguard yourself against this is to contact the British Franchise Association. Their address is 75a Bell Street, Henley-on-Thames, Oxon RG9 2BG (telephone 0491 578049). They will supply you with what is known as a Franchisee Pack, listing companies who currently have franchises available in particular areas. You can be sure that the companies the BFA list are bona fide.

9 Selling and marketing

During the formation of a business venture, selling and marketing can often play a low profile. So concerned are people to perfect their product or service, acquire the right premises, tools and staff, that actually selling what they have to offer may come very low on the agenda. This is a terrible mistake – indeed, I would go so far as to say that selling should be your first priority and that until you have proved the sale-worthiness of your product or service you should make no financial commitment at all to your venture. Let us consider the various aspects of selling and marketing in detail.

Selling

Selling is simply a question of persuading people that they want what you have to offer at a price that is mutually acceptable. There is much talk about the mysteries of selling technique and, of course, some people find it easy to sell, while others find it a strain. However, whilst you might not have the necessary skill or, indeed, qualifications to find yourself a top job as a salesman, it does not mean that you will not be able to sell your own product or service. To start with, you have a major advantage – when it comes to the nature of your product or service, you really know what you are talking about, which cannot be said of many salesmen. You know how much you can slash the price for a big order, you know how long it will take to deliver, you know precisely how the goods are made and so on. Most people are fascinated by a new business and anxious to help if you can genuinely offer value for money. As the proprietor and founder of a new business, you are on the inside track.

The techniques employed in selling a service or selling a profit do differ. Let us look at them in more detail:

Selling a product

Before deciding how to sell, you have to decide at whom you are going to aim your approach. If you are making a product in a manufacturing chain – one component part out of many –

They actually liked them! They even bought some!

then identifying your customer will be obvious. However, if you are selling to the consumer it is not obvious at all and the choice makes things more difficult rather than easier. Are you going to sell to retailers or wholesalers or are you going to approach the consumer direct – the right decision is vital.

Selling to the retail trade means either selling to a shop or a mail-order company. It has to be said that selling your product to an individual shop is a very time-consuming business. Unless, of course, you are lucky enough to persuade the buyer of a chain store to take your product. If you are dealing with individual shops, do not simply approach them in a haphazard way, but consider the implications of supply. If the shop is small and a number of miles from your manufacturing unit, will you ever be able to justify delivery? Is the shop obviously successful, with a large turnover or is it a back street boutique that hardly anyone ever visits? When making an approach to a shop, ring for an appointment first and see no one but the owner or manager. While you are on their premises try and study their business and understand it.

Having secured your order, do be wary about supply. Small retail outlets go bankrupt faster than any other type of business and you simply cannot afford to supply goods for which you are never going to be paid. Ask for cash on delivery, for the first few orders and, if possible, always. Do not be proud, plead poverty. If they want your goods and they are honest traders, then they will accept the position. If they become abusive, let it all wash over you – these are not people with whom you want to deal. If you are asked to produce something special – in other words you are commissioned to provide particular goods for an outlet – always ask for a percentage of payment on account – ideally 50 per cent.

When you have dreamt up a product, more than likely actually made it yourself, it is your baby and you are very proud of it and there is a tendency not to view it commercially. Remember the feeling when you received your first pay cheque – can I really be worth all this? It is the same feeling with your very own product and often there is a tendency to be so grateful that anybody actually wants it, that being paid for it is a secondary concern! Can I at this juncture remind you that you are starting your own business to make some money – and making money you will not do unless you take a business-like approach right from the very start.

Selling to larger shops or chain stores takes a little more organization, but is easily within your grasp – even as a cottage industry. Stores like Harrods and Fortnum & Mason, pride themselves on selling the best of British. Your blackberry preserve, based on Granny's old recipe and beautifully presented in an earthenware jar, could be just that. When approaching a big store or a chain, you can be sure that one of the first things they will ask you is about your production capacity. Do not be tempted to exagerate – tell the truth – but equally, there is no point in going to see the big boys until you can be sure of setting up a regular, reliable supply line.

The other aspect of selling to the retail trade is to sell direct to a mail-order company. Mail-order companies tend to deal with small producers and the buyers are often more accessible than the buyers of major stores. Companies tend to work 9 to 12 months in advance, so if you have a winter product to sell, you need to be making your approach around Christmas time for the following autumn. Mail-order companies are always looking for something different and they are also very price conscious. However, whilst you may not make a vast profit by selling to them, they tend to commit themselves, in advance, to large orders. This is very comforting and, provided you are dealing with one of the top mail-order companies, you can be confident that they are both stable and good payers.

Obviously you must have a suitable product – it must not be breakable or too big or heavy and it must photograph well. When making a presentation to a mail-order buyer, it is helpful to show, not only the product but also a photograph of the product, so the buyer can envisage how it will look on the page. If successful, the normal method of selling to a mail-order company is that you will be given an initial order and then told that once the catalogue comes out, you must be prepared to deliver repeat orders fast. Before you go to see a mail-order buyer work out how this would be achieved, so that you can answer the question when it is raised.

It is important to remember that whether you are selling to a small shop, a chain store or a mail-order company, the retail unit concerned will need to put between 100 and 150 per cent on the price of your goods when offering them to the consumer. In costing your goods, you need to keep an eye on the final price to the consumer to make sure the whole exercise is realistic. Retail outlets have very little flexibility when it comes to mark ups – their overheads are so high.

Selling to the wholesale trade

A wholesaler is a person who stands between the manufacturer and the retailer – a cash and carry is a wholesaler. To discover the wholesalers dealing in your particular type of product you need to consult your trade magazines. Wholesalers tend to deal only in bulk – they are not interested if you can only supply in ones and twos, or even tens and twenties – they are looking for hundreds. Once they set up a supply line between manufacturer and retailer, they want consistency – that is how they make their money.

Another type of wholesaling operation is the agent. Some retailers employ the services of an agent who goes round to manufacturers on behalf of the buyer to find suitable merchandise. This saves the buyer time. Making contact with an agent could bring you in considerable business.

Agents usually want a commission of between 10 and 20 per cent, wholesalers between 20 and 30 per cent but, whilst wholesalers will often buy in your goods, agents will simply set up the deal and will not handle the goods at all, nor make any kind of commitment to purchase.

You are bound to be nervous when making your initial selling approaches. Do not worry, having the adrenalin flowing is good for your performance! What is vital is that you are well prepared and that you can really answer satisfactorily the questions you will be asked. Make sure your samples are in tip-top condition, be on time for your appointment and, indeed, always make an appointment – never a cold call. Above all, be prepared to listen and if necessary adapt your product accordingly. More people fail to make a sale through their inability to listen than almost anything else. Even if your product is turned down outright, ask the buyer why and ask what he would like to have seen instead. You may well find that what he actually requires is something you can easily produce, but you will not know unless you ask.

Buyers are busy people. Do not waffle, come straight to the point on what you have to offer, how much it costs and why you feel he should be buying your goods. If he seems uncertain, suggest further samples, written quotations, anything to keep the dialogue open, and then make sure you deliver these within 36 hours.

Selling a service

It is a generalization, but in my view you have to be considerably more expert at selling a service than a product. Everyone accepts, with a product, that at times things go wrong in the manufacturing process – shoddy raw materials are responsible or one of your labour force make an error. However, if you are selling your expertise, you are expected to be consistently reliable, professional and efficient – and if you let a client down, you will not be forgiven.

The best way to sell a service is by word of mouth. Of course you can advertise and in the more competitive areas, such as staff agencies, you most certainly will have to do so. However, with many service industries, the best way to build the business is to get one or two satisfied clients, and let them do the rest for you. If you are selling a service, it is vital to remember that, as well as selling your skill, you are also selling your time. This makes your time particularly precious, so use it well and do not waste it on prevaricating potential clients.

Employing a salesman

I refer to sales*men* throughout this section because it becomes cumbersome to keep referring to both sexes. For *salesmen* though, please read *saleswomen* as well!

It may be that you decide to employ a professional salesman, either because of the growth potential of your business or because you simply cannot sell yourself. Of all the various types of staff that a business may need to find, finding a good salesman is the most difficult. In Chapter 10 we will be looking quite specifically at the joys and sorrows of employing people, so I will not attempt to cover the legislative mysteries here – here I shall cover choosing the right man or woman for the job.

In one respect at least your task is made a little easier in that if a salesman cannot sell himself to you, then he certainly is not going to be able to sell your product or service to anyone else. If you are going to make the financial commitment of taking on a salesman then, in my view, you should aim quite specifically for someone experienced. In the early days of your business, you simply do not have time to train a youngster – you need orders and you need orders fast.

Advertise through your trade magazines, to ensure that you find someone experienced in your particular industry. What should you be looking for? A pleasing appearance, neat and clean, good health, a pleasant person to talk to – these are all obvious qualities perhaps, but very important. Educationally? He does not need to be very highly qualified. In fact, if his academic qualifications are considerable, then he may be more of a thinker than a doer, and this you do not want. Good references are essential, and if you have any other members of staff, try him out on them to see what they think of him.

Salesmen are not cheap – they need a car and expenses and I would suggest a salary as well as commission – otherwise they will not remain loyal, and considerable training and time will need to be spent on them to make sure they are really involved in the day-to-day running of the business. To achieve this, you are looking at a figure of between £20,000 and £30,000 a year, so your salesman has got to be good! Bearing in mind the cost, do not be tempted to take on a salesman too early on in the life of your business. The most disastrous thing that can happen is that he can be too successful and bring in more orders than you can fulfil. You will lose him because he will become disgruntled, and you will lose potential customers, whose confidence you are unlikely to regain even when you have put your production house in order.

So, *before* you start making heavy commitments to your potential business idea, make up some samples or, in the case of a service, produce a dossier of what you intend doing, and try it out on people. If you cannot sell what you have to offer at this stage, then count yourself lucky that you found out before committing yourself to considerable amounts of time and money.

Marketing

In Chapter 4, we dealt with market research as it pertains to a business start-up, that is, the need to establish the market potential for your product or service. Here we consider both marketing and *monitoring* – having established a niche, you now have to set up a system to guard and protect your market and look for ways of expanding it. You can never relax and assume your ship has come in. To run a successful business, marketing needs to be part of your daily life.

Here are some of the areas where you should be particularly vigilant.

- start with your competitors – keep abreast of what they are doing and regularly send for their brochures. If you are selling a consumer product, visit major stores on a regular basis and see what is being sold and at what price. Use the knowledge you acquire about your competitors' products and service to strengthen your operation in the areas where the competition is most weak. Read your trade magazines thoroughly from cover to cover – however dreary they might appear. Learn from them what is going on in your industry
- suppliers are a good source of information. By virtue of the fact that they are trying hard to sell to you, they will inevitably be anxious to please and will be only too happy to gossip about their other customers. Remember, though, not to give too much away about *yourself* as gossip is a habit!
- if your trade is essentially a local one, keep abreast of local news – read the local papers, talk to shopkeepers, to your bank manager, solicitor, the vicar...

Whilst adaptability is the name of the game, you do not want to take your monitoring exercise so far that you are always changing directions. However, every change that does take place within your business should first be the subject of a thorough market appraisal. What is the point of buying a machine that can turn out double the capacity, if double the number of customers are not there? Marketing should be fundamental to every major decision and, of course, it should be used to ferret out new opportunities. Business these days is very volatile – knowing what is going on is the key to success.

Advertising

On the face of it, advertising seems the easy way to sell your goods or services. If you ask most potential entrepreneurs how they intend getting new customers, the stock answer will be *advertising*. Frankly, for the small business, I see advertising more as a last resort or certainly as a very low key adjunct to your selling and marketing programme. Advertising is very expensive, even in local newspapers. It sounds so easy: your local newspaper has a circulation of 35,000 people, your local radio station is tuned into by 150,000 people, 'I only have to make 30 sales a week', you say, 'local advertising has to be the answer.' No – or, at any rate, not necessarily. This blanket approach to selling is rarely effective and certainly not cost-effective. If you want to sell baby clothes, advertising in your local newspaper will mean of that 30,000 readers, at least 15,000 will be men, and of the 15,000 women, at least 10,000 will not have a baby in their life – probably more. So, you are paying for the privilege of reaching 30,000 people when your advertisement only applies to 2,000 or 3,000. Far better to organize market stalls outside local playgroups, advertise in school magazines, start up a party plan operated by young mums. Money spent in these ways will be money well spent.

So, I have done my best to put you off but if you still feel you need to advertise, then I would make the final point that advertising is not a substitute for any other business function and you should not advertise unless you actually have something interesting to say. In other words, channel your advertising spend into a period when you have a new product, a new shop, or you actually want something – premises, equipment, more staff. There has to be a distinct purpose to advertising in addition to simply saying 'Hi folks, I'm here!'

There are four main types of advertising:

- space taken in newspapers and magazines
- advertising by way of distributing brochures and sales leaflets
- air time on radio and television
- posters, display bins, point-of-sale material.

If you are placing small advertisements in local newspapers then, in my view, you do not need the services of an advertising agency. If, however, you are going to be advertising nationally, dealing with radio and television or launching any sort of major poster display, then it is essential to employ an agency.

The biggest impact of that Ad Campaign was the bill!

Contrary to what one might think, using an agent to book space for you does not actually cost any more than booking the space yourself. Agencies receive a 15 per cent discount from the media when they book space and this they keep as commission. If you try and book the same space direct in the media, you will be charged 15 per cent more than the rate the agency are quoted. Obviously, there will be considerable costs involved in layout, artwork, typesetting and so on, but using an agent for booking will cost no more.

When selecting an advertising agency, there is no need to think in terms of the firm needing to be London-based any more. Provincial agencies are very good these days – often more keen and hungry for business than their London equivalent and sometimes cheaper. However, location of your agency should not be the main criteria – ideally you want a firm who already has experience in your particular type of business and therefore understands the market. Do not be afraid to shop around – a list of agencies is available in a publication called *The Creative Handbook*, available from 100 St Martin's Lane, London WC2N 4A2 (telephone 01-379 7399).

A final note of caution on the subject of advertising agencies, do not let them lure you into spending too much and never agree to anything without first receiving a quotation in detail. In a fit of creative fervour, agencies are renowned for running up astronomic costs in their pursuit of excellence.

Having taken the plunge and indulged in a small advertising campaign, the question you have to ask yourself is what it has actually achieved for your business, and by achieve, I mean in actual terms of hard cash, such as orders. It is possible that, as a result of a clever advertisement, you receive a great many enquiries – but have those enquiries developed into orders? If not, they are of little worth and even if they have become orders, what sort of size of order? Next ask yourself whether the total number of orders has justified the advertising spent in the first place? Advertising agents will tell you that you cannot expect initial advertising to pay for itself. I query whether advertising ever pays for itself within the confines of a small campaign. At certain times of the year advertising may be justified, but always be very clear-headed about its benefits and make sure it is paying its way.

My views on advertising for small businesses do not extend to the Yellow Pages. If you have a consumer product or service, I think it is essential that you advertise in the Yellow Pages – it is the first thing people pick up when they are looking for something. Make your advertisement stand out as most people only look at the displays. This is definitely advertising money well spent and, no, I am not a shareholder in Yellow Pages!

One final note on advertising: do be very careful about the claims and statements you make within an advertisement or you will have the Advertising Standards Authority down on you. Advertising agents and, indeed, the media themselves, interfere with copy surprisingly little and you cannot expect them to pick up every mistake you have made. If you have any doubts about what you can and cannot say, do ring the Advertising Standards Authority who you will find most helpful.

Public relations

I have no reservations about public relations – it is a marvellous way to make your customer or client aware of your existence. It is also cheaper than advertising and far more effective. What is PR? Essentially it is the process by which you persuade the media to tell the world at large just how wonderful you and your business truly are. Think about it for a moment. If *you* place an advertisement, everyone knows that you are expounding your own virtues and whatever is said in the advertisement tends to be taken with a pinch of salt because of that fact. If, however, a *journalist* writes an editorial piece on your business achievements, someone else is endorsing the attributes of your product or service and, therefore, what he or she has to say carries a great deal more weight. The other great value of PR is that if you are on a tight budget in the early days of your business, it is essentially free. All it takes is a little work on your part – there is no big advertising spend and no risk involved.

Let us look at local PR first. Telephone the editorial department of your local newspaper, say you are starting a new business, you think they might be interested in covering the story and make an appointment, either to go and see them or invite them to come to you. Which you choose depends on what you actually have to show them. If your business is still looking fairly chaotic, you might be better to suggest meeting in a local pub. You need a story angle but it does not need to be very original. Perhaps you have been out of work for a couple of years and finally have taken the decision never to be employed again. Perhaps you were sitting on a river bank and suddenly had this brilliant idea! Embellishing the story of the birth of your business is not difficult. Make friends with the journalists, you will be needing them again, and do not assume that they are hard-headed people who are only interested in scandal, vice and chasing the Royal Family around the country. Journalists are always hungry for a good story and the achievements of a small business is a good story. If possible, present them with some black and white photographs of you, your product, your premises and your staff, if you have any, and make sure they are all captioned because, once they get back to the office, they might well end up in an unidentified heap on the desk. Once you have established contact with the journalist in question, keep him or her informed every time you make any kind of progress that could possibly form the basis of a good story. Make sure he or she is always invited to the launching of a new product, to Christmas parties... this sort of thing.

What applies to the local newspaper, also applies to the local TV and radio. Radio is usually quite easy to break into. Listen to your local radio station, choose a presenter you feel is most likely to be interested in what you are doing and then simply write to him or her. You are almost certain to be given an interview if you make the story interesting. TV is more difficult because there are so many demands on air time, but even if your letters are ignored initially, keep trying, and when you write to them do enclose press cuttings of any stories written about you in the local press. Try and make friends with these people and you will be sure of good and regular coverage.

So far as national PR is concerned, in my view you do need professional help to achieve it, except where specialist publications are concerned. When I ran a company making children's clothes, I found no difficulty in obtaining PR coverage in the magazines *Mother, Mother &*

Baby and *Parents*, but I could not break into such publications as the *Daily Mail* or *Woman* or *Woman's Own*. Certainly if you are selling a non-consumer product direct to industry, the comments I have made about local PR apply equally well to your trade magazine. Get to know the appropriate journalist and keep plugging away with stories.

If you have a business that you feel deserves a mention in the national newspapers or an interview with Wogan then you need the assistance of a public relations consultant. On the whole, the sort of money that will be expected from you for the services of a PR consultant is a great deal nearer the kind of budget you are likely to have available as a small business than the average advertising budget. Normally, a PR consultant will take a brief from you and then suggest that he or she is retained on a monthly basis – either over a specific period to, say, launch a new product or on a continuing basis if you feel that PR should play an ongoing role in your business activities. The fee PR consultants charge can vary from a few hundred pounds a month to a few thousand, according to what they do for you. If they feel your business is easy to promote, you may well find you can retain a PR consultant for as little as £200 to £300 a month, plus their expenses, which might sound expensive, but you can hardly buy a display advertisement in a local newspaper for that.

To find a good PR agent you should study what is called the *Hollis Press and Public Relations Annual*, which you can obtain from Contact House, Sunbury-on-Thames, Middlesex T16 5HG (telephone: 09327 84781). As with advertising agencies, try and find a PR consultant who already has some experience of your particular industry. One- and two-man bands, in my view, are usually better than large PR companies – they need your custom more.

If you are engaging in a major national PR campaign, you will need a press-cutting service. Your PR consultants will be able to tell you about this and it is not expensive. Essentially, it is important that you build up a portfolio of press coverage that can be used in a number of ways to impress potential customers, bank managers and the like. Your press cuttings need to be nicely presented in a bound folder and a press-cutting service will make sure you receive every one – whether it is a double page spread from *The Sunday Times*, or a short single column in some obscure local newspaper.

Another advantage of PR is that it will help you test the media without risking any major outlay of cash.

A personal case history When I ran a mail-order business, I wanted to take us into Sunday supplement advertising but I did not know which Sunday supplement to go for. At the time there was just the three – The Sunday Times, The Observer *and* The Sunday Telegraph. *My advertising agent strongly advised* The Sunday Times *and I was all set to follow his advice. Then, within a matter of a few weeks and by complete coincidence, I received editorial coverage in both* The Observer *and* The Sunday Times *and the response from* The Observer *was, by a long way, the better of the two. Against my advertising agent's advice, I placed my first advertisement in* The Observer *colour supplement and took £80,000 worth of orders as a result. Thereafter, consistently over the years, I found that* The Observer *attracted far more customers than* The Sunday Times *– for me (I hasten to add that this was just* my *experience in* my *particular business but, obviously, in other businesses, it could well be the other way round).*

The lesson to be learnt, however, is that PR is a good way to test the media, before committing yourself to a heavy advertising spend.

You need courage and resourcefulness to promote and sell your own product or service. Rejection, particularly in the early days of your business, is very discouraging and it is easy to become disheartened to the point where you give up altogether. If sales are slow or nonexistent, maybe you have picked the wrong kind of enterprise or perhaps there is something wrong with your product or you are charging too much? Thorough market research should tell you what is wrong and, once you recognize the problem, you can put it right and try again. Selling and marketing is only really a question of common sense. No business can have a better ambassador than its founder – the enthusiasm and commitment you can generate vastly outshines any so-called selling technique. You just need a little courage and a lot of perseverance.

10 Day-to-day running

The administrative side of a business is usally looked upon as nothing more nor less than a chore. Clearly, if you hate paperwork and are not numerate then you probably glaze over at the mere thought of keeping a set of books. Yet plotting and controlling the progress of your business can also be enormously rewarding and, contrary to what you may imagine, not particularly time-consuming. Let us look at the various aspects of controls, administration and the day-to-day running of a business.

Book-keeping

Book-keeping falls into two basic categories. There are certain internal controls that are entirely necessary for your own benefit – and which you must have the self-discipline to maintain – and there are also those controls that are visited upon you, whether you like it or not! Let us look first at the very minimum requirement for dealing with the outside world – in other words, those controls you cannot avoid.

Keeping control at the bank

At all times, you must know the state of your bank balance and you should do this by means of a cash book. On one side of the cash book you record your receipts, on the other your payments. Your cash book should be written up daily and a balance drawn so that you know precisely where you are. When your bank statement comes in, you should reconcile it against the cash book by ticking off each payment and receipt. Inevitably, there will be items on the bank statement that you have not recorded in the cash book – such as standing orders, bank charges and interest – and it is important to pick these up as they occur. If you have a large number of cheques, then you should ask the bank to supply you with weekly statements and, however small your business, you should never have anything less than a monthly statement.

If you lose track of your balance, your whole business goes out of gear. You may issue cheques against non-existent funds or you may miss opportunities by not realizing you have additional cash available. Your bank account is the nerve centre of your business and must be referred to on a daily basis.

Customers

If your sales to customers are on a cash basis only then, clearly, there may be no individual record of the sale – you will simply record the day's takings, which will equal the day's bankings. If, however, you are offering credit terms, it is vital that you have a means of keeping track of invoices to ensure that you are paid on time. At its simplest, it is a question of having two files – a file of *unpaid invoices* and a file of *paid invoices*. When an invoice is paid, you transfer it from the unpaid to the paid. This works well while your business is small. If you start to build a substantial volume of sales invoices, you need a sales journal to list and analyse your sales and a sales ledger to record the sales to each customer.

I cannot stress enough the importance of good sales records for, unless you have them up to date and properly recorded, you will become slack about collecting money and you just cannot afford to do this. Customers must pay you on time and, if they do not, you must chase them mercilessly until they do. You cannot afford to give extended credit. Invoice your customers the moment goods have been delivered and expect payment 30 days from that date. If you do not get it, scream and yell on a daily basis until you do – he who screams loudest gets paid first. You are entitled to make a fuss if you are not paid on time. You may worry about hurting your customer relationship but normally the person you sell to will not be the person in charge of accounts. Even if they are, you do not want to deal with somebody who will not pay on time. Only accurate records will ensure you keep control of this, the very lifeblood of your business.

Suppliers

As with your sales invoices, you only require two files for dealing with your suppliers, unless you are dealing with a large number of purchases. In one file you need to place the purchase invoices you have paid and in the other, the purchase invoices you have not. As you pay each invoice, you transfer it into the paid file. If you have a great many orders then you will need a purchase journal and a purchase ledger. The purchase ledger will need to be checked against suppliers' statements at least monthly.

With suppliers, your attitude should be precisely the reverse of your attitude to your customers – you should not be in a hurry to pay, unless you have promised so to do. I am not for a moment suggesting that you run up debts or let people down but, if you are dealing with a large company, always pay when a statement arrives rather than against an invoice. When reconciling the statement against your ledger, if you find they have undercharged, always pay the lesser amount – it is their mistake, let them find it. This slightly cavalier attitude to suppliers is fine when you have money in the bank, but if you are short of money then the reverse should apply. If you know you are not going to be able to pay a supplier on time then ring him up and tell him so. As a matter of courtesy this will ensure that he can make adjustments to his own cash flow, but in a practical sense, it will also indicate that, although you are having temporary problems, you are essentially an honest person who will eventually pay up. Nonpayment of an account and total silence as to the whereabouts of the cash understandably makes suppliers very twitchy.

Tax

If you are employing people then it will be necessary to have a relationship both with the Inland Revenue and the DHSS, with regard to tax and National Insurance. Surprisingly, perhaps, both bodies are really very helpful when it comes to setting up a new business. Go along and see them and they will give you all the necessary forms and advice to help you set up your first payroll. If you are intending employing a number of people, it could be sensible to consider sub-contracting your payroll to a computer bureau or, indeed, buying a small computer to handle your payroll – more of computers in the next section. Alternatively, if you employ, say, half a dozen people it might be an idea to invest in a multicopy payroll system.

VAT

Whilst we have looked at VAT and its implications in some detail in Chapter 6, it is essential to emphasize the importance of keeping an up-to-date record of sales and purchases, whether in the form of a ledger or simply in the files, so that you can quickly and easily complete your VAT return each quarter. Here again, do contact the VAT office and ask for help in administering VAT.

In looking at the simplest form of book-keeping, this represents the only relationship you must have with the outside world, unless, of course, you have a limited company, in which case you are required to have your accounts audited on an annual basis and submitted to the registrar of companies. However you would be very unwise to ignore the internal controls every properly run business needs, and these are the main areas of major concern, for the very reason that they are 'optional'.

Performance

In Chapter 5 we dealt with the preparation of a profit plan and cash forecast, so that you know what your business ought to achieve. Once you start trading, you have to compare that plan with what you *actually* achieve. Take the basic format of the profit plan and plot two columns of figures under each month – one set of figures you enter are those you prepared for your profit plan and you head them up 'PLAN'. Beside them slot in a second set of figures and call them 'ACTUAL'. This will then tell you, on a month-by-month, item-by-item basis, precisely how your business is doing as compared with its expectations. Obviously, in order to complete this form you do need to keep your other records up-to-date and this, in itself, is good for self-discipline. It may be that your backer or banker may actually require to see management accounts each month and this form will serve as an ideal way in which to present them.

Measuring performance, though, should not end with profit, there are other pieces of information you need to keep tabs upon. How many orders did you receive last week, how many enquiries, how much does that rather suspect customer owe you, why are transport costs so much higher this month? Being able to answer these questions is a vital part of being in control of your business. If you do not know what is going on, you cannot take advantage of opportunities nor put things right when they go wrong.

Stock

If you have a limited company, then once a year your auditors will require that you carry out a full stock check in order to complete the audited accounts. If you are running your business as a sole trader or partnership, there is no requirement for you to ever take stock and this can be very dangerous indeed.

Stock can be a killer to an otherwise thriving business. Too much of the wrong stock can take a strangle-hold on your business – drying up your cash flow, filling your warehouse and, in the end, making it impossible for you to continue trading. Stock must be controlled. If you have the requirement for a large turnover of stock, then you need someone responsible for checking stock in and out reporting directly to you where build ups of stock are occuring. Far too much emphasis is placed on the security aspect of stock. Of course if you are dealing in alcohol or gold bars, you do have real security problems. However for most industrial components, having a few items taken by staff on a regular basis, whilst undesirable, is not the end of the world. No, the problem lies not with security, but with the slow, insidious build up of stock, which if neglected, will in effect stagnate into a great mass of out-of-date, slow moving and, in many cases, quite unsaleable goods.

If I sound paranoid it is probably because I have had a mail-order business, where stock represents the biggest headache of all.

If you feel your stock is too small or of such a low value that you cannot justify keeping control of it on a day-to-day basis by having a storeman and detailed stock records, then do at least hold quarterly stock checks. If the value of your stock is increasing, but your sales are not, something is very wrong – somehow you are building up a stockholding you do not require. Cut your losses and get rid of the dead wood – it is no use holding on in the belief that one day you will realize the full value. If your stock is too high and you are tight at the bank, sell or somehow get rid of your dead stock – quickly.

Costings

What should your attitude to costings be – should the price you charge be aimed at undercutting the competition or should you decide you have to make a certain amount and price your goods or service accordingly.

Your pricing policy should be aimed at what the market will stand. If this means you can make an outrageous profit – congratulations, laugh all the way to the bank and think yourself very lucky. If, on the other hand, the current market price means you can barely make a profit, you need to think again – if you cannot lower your costs, can you be seen to be offering the customer something extra that justifies the high price.

Either way, costings are an essential part of day-to-day business life. You must not guess or estimate your costs.

You must know precisely what everything you sell costs down to the last penny. If you are in manufacturing, then you must consider not only the cost of raw materials and labour but also packaging and transport. A wholesaler or retailer, in theory, only has to look at the difference between his buying and selling price, but there are other factors – breakages, wastage, shelf-life – losses of this sort should be calculated on a percentage basis and applied to the costings. If you are offering a service, then time will be your prime cost, but remember time spent in travelling and any out-of-pocket expenses directly related to the job.

Do your costings regularly, watch suppliers' invoices for price increases (they certainly do not always advise you in advance) and remember you simply cannot sell *anything* unless you know what it cost.

Simple, isn't it, when you break down the various requirements of adequate book-keeping? It only really becomes a trauma when it falls behind. From the very first day of your business, bully yourself into keeping your records up to date and then, I promise you, far from being a ghastly chore, you will come to enjoy keeping a record of your achievements.

Computers

When I wrote my first small business guide book, six or seven years ago, it did not even have a section on computers. Now I think it would be fair to say that no book on business is complete without covering the subject.

Computers have totally revolutionized the business world – they have taken the chore out of a great many mundane tasks and have made the exchange of information and the analysis of progress constantly available. However, computers have their dangers too. There is a tendency to feel that a computer will solve problems, whereas in fact it is more likely to create them. I have spoken to many people running small businesses whose main pride and joy seems to be their computer system, to such an extent that you cannot help feeling that their actual business activity is almost an adjunct to it. Certainly, I think it is not an unrealistic comment to make that getting to grips with a computer can well take one's eye off the ball when it comes to looking at the priorities of both starting and running a business.

There are exceptions, of course. I have a friend who is an indexer. Very shortly after starting her business, she acquired a word processor, with special indexing software and is able to handle her work in half the time, which means she does double the work. If you are setting up an agency offering secretarial services, then it will be essential to be able to offer the services of a word processor. However, if you are looking at a computer to handle your basic business functions, I would honestly suggest that you do not consider it initially unless you personally have considerable experience as a computer user. Initially, I believe you should set up a basic manual book-keeping system and concentrate on seeing it running efficiently. Being able to feel and touch what is going on in the early days is vital. Struggling with programmes will tend to isolate you from your records, just at a time when you need constant reference to them.

The time at which I would consider the purchase of a computer is justified is when you recognize that you need someone to come and help you run the administration and accounts of your business. At this point, you can decide whether that someone is in fact a person or a computer – given a choice, I would go for the computer.

What exactly is a computer system? It is a combination of three elements:

- **Hardware**
This is the actual equipment, which normally comprises a central processor, a keyboard, a VDU (visual display unit, that is, a TV screen) and a printer. In small systems, the VDU very often incorporates the processor function

- **Software**
This is the programme that makes the computer work and you can buy different types of software for different types of functions – a payroll system, a sales ledger, a word processor, stock control – there are any number of commercial software packages and unless your business is extremely complex, there will be a package for you. You can have your own software package developed for you, but I would not recommend this until you are very familiar with computer systems for 'custom-built' packages come expensive and so they need to be just right.

- **The back up service**
When buying any piece of equipment, there must be some form of back up service if things go wrong – with a computer, this is absolutely vital. Computers are complicated things and it is not just your inability to grasp how they work that may cause problems – there are always bugs somewhere in the system. For this reason, it is sensible to purchase your computer from a local source so that there is someone on hand to help you when everything grinds to a halt – which it will from time to time!

What to look for and how to find it

Before even considering what sort of computer you need, the first thing you should do is sit down and write out a list of all functions you would like the computer to do for you, in an ideal world. This should include all the information you intend feeding into it, including an indication as to volume. You also need to calculate the likely total capacity of information you will want stored and what sort of information you will want back and, very important, how often. Do not try to write this out in any kind of computer jargon. At this stage, what you need to analyse is purely the sort of information you feel would be of benefit to your business.

Once you have a brief, you then need to decide whether you are going to approach a computer supplier direct or whether you are going to employ the services of a computer consultant to find precisely the right equipment for you. If you are going to make the approach yourself, do bear in mind that software is far more important than hardware. There are any number of different types of hardware that will do a suitable job for you, but the software package is everything. It is the software that is, if you like, the brain. The other important aspect of software is to make sure the company with whom you are dealing is not likely to go bust. One hears a number of horror stories of people who have invested tens of thousands of pounds in a computer system only to have the software supplier go out of business and so be left with a broken down system. Because computerization is still a relatively new industry and because it changes so much, so often, the brains behind new software packages are coming out of the woodwork all the time. Like all boffins, because they may be very bright at putting together a programme, it does not necessarily mean that they are very commercial.

Make sure the supplier you deal with is prepared to give you a really long-term service back up and training in the early days and do make sure that you obtain written guarantees from the supplier to the effect that he has provided you with what you specified on your brief. A computer is no simple toy after all and, until you get it up and working, you really will not know whether what you have purchased is what you actually wanted.

If you know nothing about computers then probably it would be well worth considering employing the services of a consultant. You can contact the Association of Professional Computer Consultants at 109 Baker Street, London W1M 2BH (telephone: 01-267 7144). They should be able to give you specific advice as to finding the right consultant and it is probably also sensible to mention your need to your bank manager, accountant or solicitor, who may well have a local person they can bring in to help you.

A final note on the subject of computers. There are government grants available to encourage the use of computers in industry. Have a word with the small firms division of the Department of Trade and Industry and see what is available.

Employing people

In today's climate of mass unemployment, if you are running your own business, it is tempting to suggest that you are almost duty bound to consider the employment of others. There is also the thought that, since so many people are out of work, acquiring the right person at the right price should not prove difficult. However, taking on staff should not be a decision taken lightly. It is very easy to hire but it is very difficult to fire and, between the two, within the confines of a small business, the wrong employee can cause a wealth of frustration and drama along the way.

The first question you need to ask yourself is whether the extra work load in fact could be undertaken by a machine – frankly, if so, the machine is the better option. If a machine will not do the job then consider whether your requirement for staff is a permanent and continuous one or whether what you really need is part-time or temporary help to see you through a busy time of the year. Hiring someone on a part-time or temporary basis is easy provided that you make it clear from the beginning that these are the circumstances. Taking on someone for what they imagine is going to be a full-time job, and then having to reduce it to shorter hours, will cause trouble. Let us break down the various aspects of employing people.

Recruitment

Having recognized your requirement for staff, it is tempting to leap along to the nearest employment agency and lodge your requirement. I would not. Employment agencies are expensive and a lot of them are not very professional. Having carefully outlined your requirement, you are as likely as not to be sent a great many people to interview who are entirely unsuitable and in no way meet your specification. At the end of the day, when you come to hire one of the applicants sent, you are then landed with a fee equivalent to something between two weeks' and two months' pay.

In my view, it is far better to advertise. If you are looking for local, relatively unskilled help then you cannot beat your local paper. If you are looking for someone with quite specific experience in a particular trade, then go for your trade magazine. If you want someone in top management or a highly qualified professional then I would suggest that the *Daily Telegraph* is probably your best bet. Whichever publication you choose you will find that it will work out a great deal cheaper in both time and money than using an agency – and far more effective.

Plan your advertisement very carefully – if your applicant needs to be a car driver then say so. If they need a quite specific skill and you are not prepared to compromise, say that too. Try and pack as much into the advertisement as you can in order to deflect unsuitable candidates from applying. At the same time, do be careful of both Sex Discrimination and Race Relations Acts in stating your requirements. If you have some reason for not disclosing to existing staff that you are taking on someone new, then use a box number – otherwise quote your name and address, but not telephone number. If you are advertising in more than one publication, then quote a different department number for each advertisement, so that you know where the applicant has seen your advertisement. This will be useful when placing advertisements in the future.

As the replies start coming in, acknowledge each one by postcard, by return, except where someone is obviously unsuitable, in which case send an immediate letter of rejection. When you feel you have received all likely applications, sit down and study them carefully. This may sound an over-simplification but I put a lot of store by handwriting and the presentation of a letter and, of course, more important, is what the people actually have to say about themselves. Prepare a short list and then arrange for interviews.

The interview

Never see more than three or four people in any one day because interviewing is a wearing process and you will become too tired to concentrate properly. Do not see your most likely candidate either first or last – put him or her somewhere in the middle. Job interviews are generally awful for the *interviewee* but you will find it is just as daunting being the *interviewer!* Everyone is on their best behaviour and, while this is the case, it is very difficult for either of you to judge the other. To try and combat the tension, make the surroundings and atmosphere as informal as possible. Avoid, at all costs, sitting behind a desk. Organize tea or coffee and, whatever your private views on smoking, invite applicants to smoke if they so wish. If you feel the interview is going well and the applicant could be right for the job, then extend the interview to a snack at the pub, if you can. The more relaxed your applicants are the more you will find out about them and the more likely you are to make the right choice.

Before seeing any applicants, do prepare a list of questions. It is very easy to leave out something vital unless you have a check-list to work against. Make sure before the applicant comes in that you have recently studied their track record and have made a note of one or two pertinent questions to ask. Be a good listener. Although it is important to explain both the job and your business to your potential applicant, it is far more important for you to listen to what they have to say about themselves. If you are already employing someone, do introduce them to your applicant and then *leave them alone*. You can compare notes with your existing member of staff later, but you may well find that your applicant is a great deal more at ease with someone who is not going to make the final decision about employment and therefore you may learn a lot more from a conversation with someone other than yourself. Be wary of someone who changes jobs frequently, however good the excuse. Never, never employ anybody who speaks ill of existing or past employers. Do not mind calling applicants back to interview two or three times, if you are not sure about them or if you are going through a process of short-listing, but in these circumstances, it is only fair to pay their travelling expenses.

Finally, it may seem obvious but it is very important – do not ever employ somebody you do not like.

Contracts of employment

Having decided on your member of staff, you must issue them with a contract of employment. By law, everyone who works for more than 16 hours a week should be issued with a contract of employment within 13 weeks of commencement of employment. Frankly though, anyone working for you for 16 hours or less, should have a contract of employment for this cuts out the possibilities of misunderstanding and resentment. A contract of employment does not need to be an awesome-looking document. A letter is quite sufficient, with a second copy that the applicant should sign and return as an indication of acceptance of the conditions. The contract of employment should carry the following minimum details:

- date of commencement
- title of job
- normal hours of work and any overtime arrangements
- holiday entitlement and sickness conditions

THE INTERVIEW

- position of holiday pay on termination
- notice required
- remuneration at time of employment
- details of other benefits (such as company car, pension scheme).

As with a partnership agreement, in the ideal employer/employee relationship, once the contract of employment is signed, it will be filed and never referred to again, but it is there, if something goes wrong.

PAYE and National Insurance

If you employ anyone, the salary you pay them is liable to tax under schedule E of the Income Tax Act. If you have formed a limited company, you are no longer a sole trader and so you are regarded as an employee just like the rest of your staff. It does not matter what you call yourself – director, manager, chairman, you are still an employee. The UK fiscal year ends on 5 April and, therefore, the tax deducted by you from your employees' wages and salaries is calculated up to the fifth day of each month and must be paid over to the Inspector of Taxes by the nineteenth day of that same month.

Operating a PAYE system is time-consuming and irritating, but, apart from the fact that it costs you time, it is important to remember that it is not a tax on your business – you are simply acting on behalf of the Collector of Taxes by deducting the tax due by your employees, and handing it over to the Inland Revenue. Having said that, if you fail to deduct PAYE from any remuneration you pay that is properly subject to tax, you will be charged for that tax and you may have to pay an additional penalty. Similarly, you can be in very severe trouble if you collect money from your employees and then do not pay it over to the Inland Revenue, for, in effect, you are keeping money that is not yours. For this reason, as with VAT, however tight your cash flow, always pay PAYE and VAT on time.

When an employee joins you, he or she will bring a form P45, which shows National Insurance number, current tax code and other taxation details. If, for some reason, the P45 has been lost or your new employee has not worked for a long time and does not have one, then you will have to inform the tax office, and in the meantime apply what is known as an emergency tax code number. Even if the person you are employing is going to be earning a great deal less than the standard personal allowance, you cannot simply ignore the situation for tax purposes. You will have to obtain from the employee a signed Form P46, which declares that the job with you is his or her only or main job. This ensures that you will be covered in the event of a PAYE inspection, but you must still keep a record of your employee's earnings in case details are required at some future time.

In contrast to PAYE, National Insurance is a form of taxation on the employer as well as the employee. The detailed rates have been set out in Chapter 6, but at this stage just remember that National Insurance contributions can add over 10 per cent to the cost of employing somebody! The administration of National Insurance, statutory sick pay and statutory maternity pay falls on

137

you, the employer, and this time you are working on behalf of the DHSS, rather than the Inland Revenue. Most administrative records are actually run as part of the overall PAYE system, however, and this includes payment of the monthly amounts due.

As mentioned previously, both the Inland Revenue and the DHSS are extremely helpful to the new business and will make sure that you understand how to operate the PAYE and National Insurance systems.

Dismissal

Quite rightly, there is a fair amount of legislation surrounding the dismissal of staff these days, and running foul of the system and being sued for unfair dismissal can be an expensive business. Having said that, industrial tribunals are somewhat more lenient than they were when it comes to the small business – recognizing that if someone has been dismissed, say, because he or she has proved unsuitable for a job, a small business cannot be expected to provide re-employment in a different capacity. Nonetheless, it is important to follow the rules to avoid trouble and they are these:

- every member of your staff, part-time or otherwise, who has been employed by you for *52 weeks* (or, in the case of a small business employing less than 20 people, *two years*) must be given a written statement of your reasons for dismissal

- if you wish to dismiss someone who has been with you for more than a *year* (or *two years* in the case of a small business) for some sort of unsatisfactory conduct or performance you must have given three written warnings

- the three written warnings should state very clearly why your employee is not coming up to scratch and what needs to be done to put things right. After three written warnings, if there has been no improvement in conduct, then dismissal may take place, but the member of staff may still try to take you to an industrial tribunal

- so far as period of notice is concerned, obviously this may be spelled out in a contract of employment, in which case you must adhere to it. If there is no contract of employment then you must give your employee one week's notice or a week's payment in lieu if he or she has been with you continuously for four weeks or more. After two years, you must give your member of staff one week's notice or payment in lieu for every year of continuous employment. Whilst these are the standard rates, employers often pay way over the legal requirement in order to avoid any repercussions.

Redundancy

Redundancy can only exist where a job ceases to exist. In other words, you cannot make somebody redundant one month and then employ someone in a similar capacity the following month. Redundancy payment is based on a formula relating to the length of service and rate of pay of an employee. An employee is only eligible for redundancy if he or she has been employed continuously by you for two years since the age of 18, and has not yet reached retirement age. The redundancy payment is a lump sum of compensation for the loss of a job. If you are a small business employing fewer than ten people, approximately half of the redundancy payment you make is recoverable from the Department of Employment *but only if you notify them in advance of making the redundancy.* A genuine redundancy cannot attract a claim for unfair dismissal, but make sure it is genuine. If your former employee finds out that you have taken on someone else in a similar capacity, he or she has every right to take you to a tribunal.

Having held forth on the pitfalls of employing people, I have to say that it is enormously satisfying to feel that you have developed a business to the point where it can provide someone other than yourself with employment. To be in a position to offer somebody a job, one they would not have without you, is a good feeling. Just make sure you do it right.

Professional advisers

In operating a business it is likely that you will need the help of a professional adviser from time to time. Whilst professionals cost money, they can save you a great deal, too, and can be an invaluable help in the early days of a business. Let us look at the various professions:

The solicitor

Solicitors are not cheap and, as a general rule of thumb, you should only engage the services of one when you want something quite specific done – you are buying or leasing a property, setting up a company, suing a customer who has not paid your bill, organizing a loan agreement and so on. Remember that every time a solicitor lifts the telephone or puts pen to paper, he charges you for it. Having said that, a solicitor can play a very important part in the inception of a business. A good solicitor will offer good advice, put you in touch with helpful contacts and, in acting on your behalf in negotiation, will give you a possibly quite erroneous sense of respectability! Always be frank with solicitors – nothing shocks them, they have seen it all before for their job is dealing with other people's problems. As to choosing one, personal contact is best. Failing that, choose someone you like and instinctively trust and do not be afraid to shop around.

The accountant

It may be that you do not need an accountant, particularly if you are a sole trader having a direct relationship with the Inspector of Taxes. On the other hand, if you have no personal experience of accounts and you feel you are rapidly losing control, the sooner you bring in an accountant the better. There are various people around, who can best be described as self-styled accountants – in other words they are not qualified – and you want nothing to do with these. Anyone you use should be a member of the Institute of Chartered Accountants or the Association of Certified and Corporate Accountants. Accountants, like solicitors, are expensive. In asking for their help, try and do as much spade work for them as possible. Although you can throw them an envelope full of jumbled invoices and a few cheque stubs and they will sort them out for you, they will do so for a price, so present your accounts in such a way that there is the very minimum to do. In choosing a firm of accountants, again personal contact is best, but if neither your bank manager nor solicitor can introduce you to someone (which is very unlikely) then look to a small firm who are inclined to give you the personal attention you need.

The bank manager

We have looked at banks in relation to borrowing money, but they do have many other things to offer besides hard cash! Your bank manager is in touch with local traders, local professional people and financial institutions and he has his finger on the pulse of what is going on in the world of money and commerce. Chewing over the problems of your business with a bank manager is entirely free – not so with an accountant or a solicitor.

Just one word of caution in seeking your bank manager's advice – do remember that he is not likely to have actually run a business – all his advice is based on second-hand knowledge.

The insurance broker

This is a really important person in your life, whose fees are also gloriously non existent! More of him in the next section on insurance.

The estate agent

If you are selling a property, you need an estate agent. If you are buying one, you do not. I do not think much of estate agents. The advice they give is always tempered by how much they can make out of you and the time and trouble they tend to take with clients in no way reflects the enormity of the fee. Harsh judgement, yes, but if you are seeking premises, never commission an estate agent – simply obtain all the agents details you can, check the local papers and tramp around the area yourself.

The consultant

Business consultancy is quite big business. There are some good consultants but there are an awful lot of con men as well. You do not *need* a consultant – you have your bank manager, your solicitor, possibly your accountant, your family, your friends – if you need to talk, they can listen to your problems and give you a balanced view. The one possible exception to this is the computer consultant. As this is such a specialist area and you are considering spending big money on a computer, then I would recommend you consider taking advice from an independent consultant – otherwise do not touch them with a barge pole.

In your dealings with the professionals never lose sight of the fact that you are the client. They can be a fairly intimidating bunch and are quite likely to blind you with science.

You are the boss and do not forget it. Remember, too, that their advice is not necessarily right and that in your dealings with them you should always stand back slightly from what you are being told, make your own analysis of the situation and compare what you instinctively feel with what you are being told. Of course, in some complicated legal tangles or high-powered financing, you may have to rely very heavily on the advice of the professionals, but stay on top and stay in charge. If you do not understand what they are saying, get them to say it again. It is your business, you are taking the risks, when all is said and done, you are the final judge and jury, and you are paying the bill. Just remember the dog should wag the tail.

Insurance

If you are thinking of going into business, and currently simply have normal domestic insurance, then whatever the intended size of your business, you are going to have to re-appraise your insurance cover. No, not just sometime – *before* you actually start trading. It really is important because once you go commercial, you can come very unstuck if you are not adequately covered.

Taking a business at its most basic

– you employ no one, you are making a simple product in your own home and surely, you say, I do not need any insurance cover? Yes, you do. As we discussed under business property, the moment you carry on any form of business within your own home, your householder's policy will no longer cover your activities. True to say, if you are knitting sweaters, a ball of wool rolls into the fire, your are too tired to notice it has happened and the place burns down, the insurance company is going to have a devil of a job proving it was while you were in the midst of commercial knitting that the tragedy happened. Nonetheless, they might be able to and it is simply not worth the risk. If the activity you are undertaking is not a serious fire risk, there will be very little alteration in your premium, but at least the insurance company have been notified and cannot come back on you if, inadvertently, your commercial venture causes a catastrophe. If, however, your business is a quite recognizable fire hazard – candle making, something involving a kiln, or whatever, then you need to recognize that there is going to be a fairly substantial increase in premium. Still it is worth it – to lose your home and then find you are only partially covered would be complete disaster.

The other type of insurance you must consider – and it is not expensive – is *public liability*. If you are offering a consumer product or service, you need public liability cover. What happens if your pot of home-made chutney poisons somebody or you are painting someone's house and accidently drop the paint pot on the head of a passerby – *you* are liable and the claim could prove very expensive. Public liability insurance is a must if you are providing either a product or service to the consumer.

A personal case history *When I ran my children's clothes business I supplied many thousands of polyester/cotton tartan shirts. They were very popular and we sold them in the same style and pattern over a number of years. One day, I received a call from a solicitor to say that a writ was in the post because one of my shirts had caught fire and a child had been very badly burned as a reult. I was appalled, as you can imagine. The child in question was only two – the same age as my own daughter at the time – and the thought that I might have produced something that had inadvertently caused this child's injuries was horrifying – in other words, I was immediately thrown into a highly emotional state. I was insured. I rang my insurance broker who said to leave the matter in his hands and he would sort it out. The insurance company quickly got to the bottom of the story. To start with, the polyester/cotton shirt I was* supplying was the standard polyester/cotton mix that you find in any shop and there was nothing wrong with that particular batch of fabric. The two year old in question had been helping his father light the family barbeque. He had apparently fallen over and, in an effort to save himself, had literally put his arm into the barbeque. The insurance representative, who called round to the boy's house, instantly, I believe, accurately assessed the situation. The mother of the child was absolutely livid with the father for having let the child so near the barbeque, and the father was desperately seeking someone else to blame. Of course the shirt sleeve had burnt, as would any fabric applied to red-hot coals, but there was no claim for my insurance company to answer.

Two things are relevant from this case history:

- if I had been in the wrong, I was covered by insurance
- without insurance, not only would there have been the risk of an unprotected claim, but I would have found dealing personally with the matter very distressing. As it was, once the matter was cleared up, I sent the mother a new shirt, with the company's compliments and she, in fact, continued to be a customer. The child made a full recovery.

As your business grows, you are going to need to consider other forms of insurance. People's attitude to insurance often tends to be rather wrongly geared. Too much emphasis is placed on unimportant insurance – like petty cash, office windows, pieces of equipment that have been written off years ago. Here are some of the insurance covers that you should consider as you expand.

Loss of profits

No company can afford to spend a fortune on insurance but the question you should ask yourself, as your business grows, is what happens if a real disaster strikes – if the factory burns down or your major supplier's factory burns down? This is where you should be concentrating your thoughts – what will be the implications on your business in these circumstances. First, there will be an immediate loss of profits and this needs to be insured against. Secondly, presumably, you do not want to lose your work force, so their wages and salaries have to be paid while the factory is rebuilt. I am not talking here just about bricks and mortar – I am talking about the implications of your suddenly not being able to trade. While you have no staff, while you are not too dependent on the income you are receiving from your business, this is not an insurance that you need to bother too much about, but the moment your business reaches the point where you and others need the income it generates, then you must insure against potential loss. This category of insurance is known under a variety of names – loss of profits, or consequential loss or, more recently, business interruption.

Employer's liability

The moment you employ someone, either full- or part-time, on or off your premises, you must take out employer's liability cover. This cover insures you against claims by employees for any injury that may take place during the carrying out of their duties, which, of course, may not necessarily take place on your premises. This insurance is not expensive unless your staff are in a particularly high-risk area, but I have to stress that, if you employ anyone, you *must* have employer's liability cover.

Professional indemnity

If you are providing a service, it is important to consider a professional indemnity policy, though I would hasten to add that this is far from cheap. Nonetheless, if you are providing advice that is materially going to affect people's lives, you have to accept that your advice, if wrong, could invite your client to sue you for compensation. Doctors, accountants, solicitors and so on automatically take out this sort of cover, so do many other professional people. It may be possible to save yourself a lot of money by joining a union. If you have a union affiliated with your particular trade, check out the position. You may find that by being a union member, you are automatically covered for professional indemnity.

Assets

If you have an asset of any worth, you need to insure it – stock, equipment, property, computers, motor vehicles, are all obvious candidates. One possible area you might overlook is *goods in transit*. They are particularly vulnerable and if you do not, quite specifically, identify the requirement for this cover, you could find that you are caught between two policies – not being on your premises, the goods are not insured and not having reached your customer's, they are not covered by their insurance either.

Do bear in mind any special risks associated with assets: if, for instance, you are in catering, then you must insure against the possibility of your freezer breaking down.

Stock is another very important aspect to consider when you are looking at insuring your assets. Losing stock has a number of implications – there is the value of the stock at cost

144

and there is a loss of profit that you would have gained from selling that stock. Insuring stock is expensive, particularly if it is easy to remove from the premises or particularly desirable. For this reason you can take out an insurance policy that allows for a monthly declaration of stock value, which ensures that month by month you are adequately, but not over-insured.

Commercial insurance may seem to you to be something of a minefield and, for this reason, when considering insurance, you should deal through an insurance broker. An insurance broker is an independent adviser working for no one particular insurance company and whose job it is to assess your requirements and then find the best possible deal for you. No, it is not expensive – miraculously, it costs nothing, for the broker earns his living from commissions paid to him by the insurance companies. Surprisingly it is not cheaper to go direct to the companies concerned because they charge a standard rate whether you deal through a broker or direct.

A good insurance broker will visit you regularly to see whether your circumstances have changed and, if they have, your policies will be altered accordingly. A broker will do all the donkey work of filling out the forms and obtaining quotations and all you have to watch is that he does not become too carried away and over-insure you. Word of mouth is the best way to find an insurance broker. I would suggest you contact your bank manager or solicitor and ask them to recommend someone to you. If you can find somebody local this is obviously best.

Being adequately insured is an essential requirement of every business. Do not go over the top, but do look at your vulnerable areas and make sure you are protected.

This chapter, then, has dealt with the main controls and administration necessary for running your business and, when broken down, it is not too arduous. Records only become a problem when they are neglected and, however small your business transactions in the early days, do set up the necessary controls for, as your business grows, you will have the systems already in operation to cope with the pressure.

11 Success and failure

Your money-making venture is going to be one of two things – a success or a failure. In theory, both aspects are easy to define: *success* is making big profits, providing a product or service that everyone wants; *failure* is going bust.

I query, however, whether success and failure can be that easily defined. What happens if your business becomes so successful that it is running *you*, rather than you running *it*? Your family life suffers, your children rarely see you except when you are tired, harrassed and preoccupied – is that success, however big the profits? To me, it sounds more like failure. Going right back to our discussions at the beginning of this book, one of the most difficult aspects of going commercial is to recognize your own limitations – either in terms of ability or in terms of commitment. If you want anything approaching a normal family life then your business is going to have to be kept in check. This means it has to be controlled and contained at a certain level, beyond which it will take you over completely.

Always keep at the very forefront of your mind the reasons why you went into business in the first place. Whilst the shape of your business activities may change and shift, your reasons for going into business will not. If you find that your business activities are straying away from those original aims, then do something about it. Let us now look at the implications of success and failure, in more detail.

Coping with expansion

Expansion is the natural progression of a successful business – up to a point. Do remember that big is not necessarily beautiful and, more especially, not necessarily profitable. If you have established a market and are meeting the demands of that market by producing a product or service, will doubling your production actually double your profits? Not necessarily, for will the market automatically double to meet your extra production? You may have already saturated the market, in which case, there are no more sales to be had, or you may have to sell further afield, thus reducing your profit margin. It is a fact that the first slice of the market is always the easiest to obtain and to both acquire and keep an increasingly large market becomes more difficult. Of course, aside from straightforward expansion, you could look at diversification. Dashing off at a tangent is not a good idea but it could be that there is an adjunct to the product or service you are currently supplying that will be relatively easy for you to produce and that could enhance your existing business. Alternatively, if you have a major supplier, is it possible that you could produce what you are buying from him yourself, thus taking your manufacturing process one stage backwards? Yet again, if you are selling your goods to a wholesaler (or a retailer come to that) you could take one or two steps forward and develop your own shop. When Terence Conran could not find anybody interested in selling his cheap and cheerful furniture, he opened his own shop. The result, of course, was Habitat.

If you can see no way of expanding your existing business, there are two alternatives.

Buying another business

You could buy out a competitor or buy a business that will take you into a new area. Finding the right business could move you into a new market sector and expand your range of products or services. However, in buying a business, you always need to consider why it is for sale in the first place. People, on the whole, are very reluctant to sell profitable businesses with a healthy-looking future. Never consider buying a business without the help of an accountant and a solicitor to thoroughly pull it apart before you commit yourself. Suffice to say here, though, it is potentially a good method of expansion.

Merging

You could consider merging your business with another. Merging means, quite literally, two businesses becoming one and, of course, this inevitably leads to all sorts of management problems. Who is going to head up the new company – you or the boss of the one with whom you are merging, what is the pecking order for your staff and his? Who is in charge of what is the major trauma involved in merging.

As a general rule, I think it is a very difficult and fraught process *merging* two businesses whose activities are identical – in such a case one should be *bought* by the other. The only way a merger is going to work successfully is if the businesses are involved in parallel activities, so that the newly formed company can feed off itself without destroying itself in the process!

There are various implications of expansion, whether it is by merger, buying or other means, that are sometimes very difficult to handle. One of the hardest areas is with regard to staff. In the early days of your business, you would probably have a small, loyal band of people who help you through thick and thin. Because you are a new business – vulnerable and short of cash – your little band will probably work all hours of the day and night, for barely adequate wages and you will all get to know one another very well. The pioneer spirit certainly does bond people together.

Thanks largely to the work of these early helpers, your business grows, orders pour in, new premises are sought and you are on the way up. Yippee! So what is your natural inclination – to reward those early helpers, to show them just how much you appreciate what they did for you in those difficult early years. And what is the most natural way of rewarding them? Promotion, higher salary, more prestigious job, more responsibilities – a natural progression and therefore, naturally, the right thing to do. Wrong. Those people who helped you in the early days were suited to being part of a cottage industry – they are therefore likely to be *doers* not *managers*. It is possible that some of them might have management potential but far more likely, they will not. Hard though it may be, as you expand, you will need to recognize that you will have to bring in management over the top of your original team. It has to be, but it is also a very difficult thing to do. I have made this mistake several times. When you over-promote people, far from rewarding them, you put a load on their backs that worries and upsets them. Of course, initially, they are very pleased with the increase in salary but, in the end, the job becomes too much. More often than not, you will lose the very person you wanted above all to reward and maintain as a member of your work force.

So, when you are looking at the expansion of your business, recognize the limitations of your staff and, above all, recognize the limitations of yourself.

Recognizing the danger signals

Most businesses fail because they do not have the resources to maintain their trade. This may be because the business had insufficient working capital to start with, because the business has been trading at a loss for longer than was expected, because it has been giving away too much credit or a variety of other reasons. Usually a combination of these factors is exaggerated by the principal playing ostrich and failing to acknowledge that all the signs are there – and, suddenly, it is too late.

The tragedy is that most of the businesses which fail, could have been made to work. All they have really suffered from is an acute case of that well-known problem – *the cash flow crisis*. When we looked at assessing your financial requirements, I did stress the need to make sure you were really adequately funded. What applies to initial funding, continues to apply throughout your business career. Expansion of any sort almost always requires additional funding – even if it is on a temporary basis – and the trick is to acquire that funding *before* your cash facilities have reached crisis point.

It is easy to do things properly. Let us assume you have been jogging along with the odd sale here and there and suddenly your first really big order lands on the desk. Excitedly, you dash out and order raw materials and take on an extra couple of part-time staff. But wait. How long is it going to be before you can fulfil this order and when is your supplier going to want to be paid? What are the extra staff going to do to your wages bill and, most importantly, is the customer going to come across with your payment? The thing to do is sit down and work all this out, apply it to your Cash Forecast and see what it does to your bank balance. I suspect you will be horrified, but you do not need to be. If you have planned for this temporary cash crisis then an approach to your bank manager *before* you commit yourself to the order, will almost certainly result in him agreeing to finance you. If he is not prepared to finance your total requirements, then you will either have to negotiate long credit terms with your supplier, work harder and manage without the temporary staff or ask your customer for payment on account. However, if you find yourself half-way through fulfilling the order, having run out of money at the bank, the manager is unlikely to extend your facilities when you are already overdrawn on your overdraft. When you ask your supplier for more time to pay, he will simply stop supplying and you cannot very well ask your customer for money on account when you are only half-way through the job. Deadlock – it is how many businesses come to grief.

Avoid cash flow problems is a question of looking, not only at what your requirements are today, but what they are likely to be tomorrow and planning accordingly. It is also a question of recognizing that you cannot achieve everything all at once, which may mean that you actually have to turn down a large order because you are not ready to cope with the financial implications.

In the early days of your business, the other classic situation you are liable to face is lack of sales. Wild with enthusiasm, you set up your workshop, take on staff and start producing like mad. Then you find that breaking into the market is not as easy as you had imagined. You have a big stock, wages to find and no money coming in – your business seems doomed before it has started. Do not panic – sell off your stock for whatever you can get for it. I know, you are going to make a huge loss, but goods are only worth what people will pay for them. Clear it all out via a market stall, a car boot sale, whatever. Sorry, but get rid of your staff, too. Then start all over again by approaching the market, seeing what they want and then making it. Survival depends on your ability to recognize when you must cut your losses. Refusing to recognize the danger signals is the quickest way to bankruptcy.

Bankruptcy, receivership and liquidation

There is usually no one single cause of business failure – it is normally a combination of events. The six main causes are these:

- cash flow problems
- lack of sales
- poor administration
- poor costings resulting in too low a profit
- bad management
- bad luck.

The terrifying thing about business failure is that it seems to speed up the nearer you get to the end. You find yourself on a sort of helter-skelter, spiralling down to disaster, and the lower you sink, the more difficult it is to climb out of the abyss. It is so very important to keep a clear head, despite the stress you are under, for taking the right decisions in these circumstances can do a lot towards minimizing failure. Let us look at the three different aspects of a business collapse.

Receivership

Receivership may not mean the end of a business. Receiverships only apply in the case of limited compaies and, what happens, in essence, when a company is in serious financial difficulty, is that the major lenders, who have the security of a debenture or mortgage, appoint a receiver who takes over the control of the company from the directors and attempts to salvage the situation. In most cases the receiver is likely to be appointed by the major bank involved. A good receiver will look at ways in which he can liquidate some of the assets, so that the bank can be repaid, without completely killing off the company. Like everything else, though, there are good and bad receivers, and if you get a bad one, all he is apparently interested in is raising enough cash to pay his fee and get out fast. This means he will sell off your assets at prices that are appallingly low and you will be left, possibly with personal guarantees and commitments, and no resources to cover them. If you are faced by the threat of receivership, rather than try and avoid it, your best bet is to influence the choice of receiver. Then, rather than look on him as the enemy, try and work with him to save your business. Contrary to what one might imagine, receivers do not have bolts through their neck – they are actually quite reasonable people, usually accountants specializing in business trauma – and their aim should be to save rather than destroy a business.

Bankruptcy

Any individual can sue another in bankruptcy. If you owe money you cannot pay and you have incurred the debt in your own name, then you may be sued, made bankrupt and sufficient of your assets sold in order to settle your debts. If you are operating as a sole trader or partnership, then you are vulnerable to bankruptcy since you do not have the protection of a limited company. If you incur business debts you cannot pay, then your personal assets – which means your house, furniture, your car – can be sold to clear those debts.

If you are in a high-risk business, it may be sensible to transfer your major family assets into someone's name. I hesitate to give this advice because it suggests that I am implying you can then take a cavalier attitude towards your debts. Being in debt is a soul-destroying thing, there is no worse thing in the world than being chased for money. Of course you should go into business with the intention of always paying your debts, but if you have a young family who need protecting, it might be better if the house, at any rate, is in your husband's name, in the early, vulnerable years of trading.

These days, if you are made bankrupt with big debts, you sometimes do not have to pay it all back before you are discharged. However, one of the worst aspects of bankruptcy – apart from the inevitable stigma – is its terrible expense. By the time all the costs have been added to your debts, you can find your total liabilities have doubled or even trebled.

So, you must avoid bankruptcy at all costs and the best way to do this is to be scrupulously honest with your suppliers. If you explain you cannot pay them and why, and then offer to pay even a few pence a week, the chances are, they will agree. People usually only sue for bankruptcy when they feel they are being duped and taken for a ride. Indeed, most people are fairly decent and, if you can persuade your supplier that you are making every effort to repay him as quickly as you can, he is not going to kick you when you are down for he is far less likely to get his money if he does.

Liquidation

Liquidation is something that happens to limited companies and what it means is that all the company's assets are disposed of and the money received is distributed on a pro rata basis amongst the general creditors, once the secured and preferential creditors have been satisfied. In other words, liquidation follows on from receivership if the receiver feels that nothing can be done to save the business.

What is meant by *secured* and *preferential creditors?* Secured creditors are likely to be bankers and financial institutions from whom you have borrowed money. When you signed up the loan agreements, they will have put a charge on your business assets that quite literally means that they have to be paid first, before any other money is distributed. Thereafter, the preferential creditors are paid and these are usually wages to staff, Inland Revenue, Customs and Excise and DHSS debts, which again have to be settled ahead of the other creditors. Only when these people are satisfied are the unsecured creditors dealt with – which means your day-to-day suppliers. Do bear in mind that if there is not sufficient money within the company to pay preferential creditors, it is possible that they may look to the directors for payment from personal resources. It is for this reason that I have stressed, all through the book, how very important it is to keep your VAT and DHSS payments up to date.

Bankruptcy, receivership, liquidation – they are emotive words that seem to represent the ultimate in failure and it is no good pretending it is not all a horrific business. The most successful way to fail is to fade out, rather than go with a bang. If you recognize that you cannot make your business work, try organizing things so that the people you have to pay are paid and that the assets are gradually disposed of to meet the most pressing debts. Certainly, if you can, wind down the business while you, yourself, are still in charge. This will minimize the trauma and will also ensure that you obtain the maximum possible from your assets. At the end of the day you may still have money owing but the sum in question will be much reduced, and the right people will have been paid off first.

A very experienced receiver I know told me that the awful thing about business failure is that most of the damage is done in the last few months before the business ultimately collapses. Instead of recognizing that there is no way out, the principals, in a desperate attempt to keep the business alive, take on still more borrowing, run up huge debts with suppliers, get behind with vital payments like VAT and PAYE – in other words, anything to keep the business alive. It is these last-ditch attempts at a rescue that make the mess at the end infinitely worse than it would have been if they had recognized earlier that there was no way out. Of course, you must fight to save your business and I do not believe that there can be a successful business in operation today, that, at some point in its development, has not been closer to failure than the principal would care to admit. It is truly heartbreaking, after the weeks, months or years of effort and enthusiasm you have put into something, to see it crumble before your eyes. But do not hang on to it at all costs – recognize that there has to be a time to let go.

Cashing in on success

How far do you want to take your business? What is the extent of your ambition? Do you want an additional income of £100 a week or do you want to be heading up a multi-million pound business quoted on the Stock Exchange? In the early days, survival is probably your main aim, but once your business is established, you need to begin formulating a plan as to exactly where you want to go with your venture. Businesses, like everything else in life, do not stand still and you need to shape the direction of your future.

If you have a teenage child who has already expressed interest in coming into the business, then you need to make it as stable as you can, so that when, eventually, you bow out and your child takes over, there is a solid foundation from which he or she can work. If you have developed your business to the point where it is ticking over nicely and providing you with just the right level of work and income, then you need to consider how long you see yourself wanting to go on in this way – five, 10, 20 years? Ultimately, though, you are going to want to stop work or do less and if you do not have a child who wants to take over the business from you, then the ultimate answer must be to sell out. This is one of the chief advantages of having your own business. Over the years a successful business should provide you with a regular income but, in addition, building a profit record, cornering a piece of the market, is establishing something that has a value. The name given to that value is *goodwill* and, ultimately, when you feel you have worked long and hard enough, your business will have a value based on the tangible assets of property, equipment, stock and so on and the goodwill you have built into it.

If you are shaping up your business for sale, it is preferable that you sell it as a limited company. In the structure of a limited company, the assets, liabilities, profits and losses are so much more clearly defined and, from the buyer's point of view, it seems far more tangible than simply taking over from a sole trader.

If you have run your business, your way, for a number of years, you probably are quite confident that you are indispensable. I have to say that you are not. If your potential buyer does not want you to stay on with the business during a hand-over period, then be supremely grateful and not in the least hurt. There is nothing worse than staying on with a business in some sort of consultancy capacity, watching someone else running the business *you* started and making changes that you consider quite wrong. Putting it in everyday terms, think about selling your house: you cannot bear the thought of what new owners would do to your home. Everyone sees things in a different light. I wonder how many times in the average, shall we say, 300-year-old cottage, the inglenook fireplace has been blocked up and then unblocked, as each new set of owners exercise their preferences. You cannot expect someone to take over your business and *not* make changes – radical changes that you will find very offensive. So, if you can get out without continuing involvement, do so.

Unfortunately, though, more likely than not, you will be asked to stay on for a period. If you have to agree to it, do so, but make it for the shortest time possible.

One aspect of selling a business that is sometimes adopted is that a buyer may suggest that part of the payment for the business is withheld until he has taken over and sees that the profits can be maintained. You cannot agree to guarantee future profits unless you also maintain a degree of control over the business. If you agree to wait for, shall we say, 25 per cent of the purchase price for 12 months and then, during the first 12 months of new ownership, the new owner makes a lot of idiotic decisions that reduce the profit, then you are going to lose out. You must either settle for nothing but full payment or be in a position to block crazy decisions that will affect profitability, until you receive your total payment.

Whatever you do, when it comes to the disposal of your business, do not be sentimental. When all is said and done, at the end of the day, it is the size of the cheque that counts.

Conclusion

Precious few of our mothers or grandmothers would have considered, even fleetingly, the possibility of a business of their own. Fifty years ago, private enterprise belonged to brilliant eccentrics with innovative ideas and industry was largely controlled by great unwieldy companies. Today it is recognized that the economy of this country depends on people like you and me, starting little money-making ventures that support us and, possibly, one or two other people, providing goods or services that are unique to us and with which no large organization or foreign importer can compete.

However good your job, however well paid, however high-powered, there is something quite unique about making a success of a money-making venture of your own. Although you will find your own business harder work than any job you have ever undertaken, the feeling of achievement is second to none.

Ask as wide a range of entrepreneurs as you like if they still remember receiving their first order. Without exception, they will be able to tell you every detail about it – however long ago it happened.

It is heady stuff, this world of private enterprise and I do hope this book will have encouraged you to try it. Women, particularly, have far greater resources to draw on than we normally give ourselves credit for. You just need a little push to take the first few tentative steps. Go on, you can do it!

Useful addresses

General

The Advertising Standards Authority
Brook House
Torrington Place
London WC1
Telephone: 01-580 5555

British Franchise Association
75a Bell Street
Henley-on-Thames
Oxon RG9 2BG
Telephone: 0491 578049

The British Overseas Trade Board
1 Victoria Street
London SW1
Telephone: 01-215 7877

CoSIRA (Council for Small Industries in Rural Areas)
141 Castle Street
Salisbury
Wiltshire SP1 3TP
Telephone: 0772 336255
(This is their head office but they also have regional offices around the country)

The Department of Employment
Administrative Headquarters –
Caxton House
Tothill Street
London SW1
Telephone: 01-213 3000

Wages Inspectorate –
Clifton House
83/117 Euston Road
London NW1 2RB
Telephone: 01-387 2511

The Department of Trade and Industry
1–19 Victoria Street
London SW1H 0ET
Telephone: 01-215 7877

Millbank Tower
Millbank
London SW1P 4QU
Telephone: 01-211 6486

English Tourist Board
Thames Tower
Blacks Road
London W69 E1
Telephone: 01-846 9000

The Guild of Glass Engravers
19 Portland Place
London W1N 4BH
Telephone: 01-580 6952

Health Education Council
78 New Oxford Street
London WC1A 1AH
Telephone: 01-637 1881

Her Majesty's Stationery Office
Orders and Enquiries –
PO Box 276
London SW8
Telephone: 01-622 3316

Retail Counter Service –
Holborn Bookshop
49 High Holborn
London WC1
Telephone: 01-928 6977

Highlands and Islands Development Board
17 Cockspur Street
London SW1
Telephone: 01-930 4004

Industrial Development Board for Northern Ireland
Head Office –
IDB House
64 Chicester Street
Belfast BT1 4JX
Northern Ireland
Telephone: 0232 233233

London Office –
Northern Ireland Business Centre
11 Berkley Street,
London W1X 6BU
Telephone: 01-493 0601

The Registrar of Companies and Limited Partnerships
Board of Trade
Companies House
55 City Road
London EC1
Telephone: 01-253 9393

Scottish Development Agency
Head Office –
120 Bothwell Street
Glasgow 2
Telephone: 041-248 2700

London Office –
17 Cockspur Street
London SW1
Telephone: 01-839 2117

Scottish Tourist Board
23 Ravelston Terrace
Edinburgh EH4 3EU
Telephone: 031-332 2433

London Office –
17 Cockspur Street
London SW1
Telephone: 01-930 8661

Small Firms Division
Abell House
John Islip Street
London SW1
Telephone: 01-212 3395
(There are also regional offices)

The Small Firms Service
Consult your telephone book for your local Freefone number

Wales Tourist Board
Brunell House
2 Fitzalan Road
Cardiff CF2 1UY
Telephone: 0222 499909

London Office –
34 Piccadilly
London W1
Telephone: 01-409 0969

Welsh Development Agency
Europe House
World Trade Centre
London E1
Telephone: 01-265 1839

Associations

The Association of Independent Computer Specialists
Leicester House
8 Leicester Street
London WC2H 7BN
Telephone: 01-437 0678

Association of Professional Computer Consultants
109 Baker Street
London W1M 2BH
Telephone: 01-267 7144

The British Hand-knitting Association
PO Box CR4
Leeds LS7 4NA
P.O. Box only – no phone

Direct Selling Association
44 Russell Square
London WC1B 4JP
Telephone: 01-580 8433

Equity British Actors
8 Harley Street
London W1
Telephone: 01-636 6367

The National Farmer's Union
Agriculture House
Knightsbridge
London SW1
Telephone: 01-235 5077

National Federation of Beauty Therapists
PO Box 36
Arundel
West Sussex BN18 0SW
Telephone: 0903 88 3027

Phonographic Performers Ltd
Ganton House
14–22 Ganton Street
London W1
Telephone: 01-437 0311

Magazines

The Draper's Record
Knightway House
20 Soho Square
London W1V 6OT
Telephone: 01-935 6611

The Grocer
5–7 Southwark Street
London SE1 1RQ
Telephone: 01-407 6981

Hollis Press and Public Relations Annual
Contact House
Sunbury-on-Thames
Middlesex T16 5HG
Telephone: 09327 84781

The Lady
40 Bedford Street
London WC2
Telephone: 01-836 8705

Books, leaflets and courses

Books and leaflets

Careers in Journalism
National Union of Journalists
314 Gray's Inn Road
London WC1X 8DP
Telephone: 01-278 7916

Code of Practice for In-home Selling
Direct Selling Association
(for their address, see page 55)

The Creative Handbook
100 St Martin's Lane
London WC2N 4AZ
Telephone: 01-379 7399

The Food Hygiene (Market Stalls and Delivery Vehicles) Regulations 1966
Health Education Council

Letting Rooms in Your Home
Department of Environment

Planning Permission – a Guide to Industry
HMSO

The Simple Methods of Candle Manufacture
Intermediate Technology Publications
9 King Street
London WC2 E8HN
Telephone: 01-836 6379

Toys (Safety) Regulations 1974
Leaflet number S1 1367
HMSO

The Wages Council Act
Department of Employment, Wages Information

The Writer's and Artist's Yearbook
A. & C. Black

Your Guide to Food and Hygiene
HMSO

Your Guide to Food Hygiene (General Regulations) 1970
HMSO and Health Education Council

Courses

- Access to Information Technology
- The Job Training Scheme
- Training for Enterprise
- The Wider Opportunities Programme

Contact your local Job Centre or Manpower Services Commission for further information about these courses.

Index

Accountants, 140
Advertising, 118–120, 134
Allowances, maternity, 82
Articles of Association, 106
Assets, 114–145
Audit, 106

Banks, 66
Bank managers, 140
Bankruptcy, 151–152
Benefits,
   child, 82
   disability, 82
   supplementary, 81
   unemployment, 80
Book-keeping, 124–130
Business expansion, 146–147
Business Expansion Scheme, 70–71
Business ideas, index of,
   acting, 43
   animal minding, 43
   antique furniture restoral, 35
   artificial flowers, 35
   bed and breakfast, 53
   beauty therapy, 43
   bookbinding, 35
   book-keeping, 49
   boutique, running a, 46
   breeding and rearing, 54
   business consultancy, 49
   cake decorating, 40
   camping and caravans, 54
   candle making, 36
   childminding, 56
   china repairs, 36
   cleaning, 50
   clothes hire, 46
   crocheting, 46
   commercial use of the home, 53–54
   computer programming, 49
   disc jockey, 43
   door-to-door selling, 55–56
   dressmaking, 47
   driving, 44
   editing, 44
   egg decorating, 36
   enamelling, 36
   frozen meals, 40
   function catering, 41
   gardening, 49
   glass engraving, 36
   growing herbs, 54
   hairdressing, 50
   home help service, 56
   interpreting, 50
   jewellery making, 36
   journalism, 44
   knitting, 47
   lampshade making, 36–37
   leatherwork, 37
   letting, flats and rooms, 53
   market gardening, 55
   market research, 50
   model making, 37
   modelling, 45
   musician, 45
   odd jobs, 45
   painting, 37
   painting and decorating, 51
   party plans, 55
   photography, 37
   picture framing, 38
   pottery, 38
   preserve making, 41
   printing and publishing, 38
   public, opening a garden to the, 54
   removals, 51
   running an agency, 48
   sandwich making, 41
   second-hand clothes, selling, 47
   snack bars and cafes, running, 42
   speculating, 53
   teaching, 51
   telephone answering, 52
   toy making, 38
   translating, 52
   upholstery making, 39
   weaving, 39
   woodwork and carpentry, 39
   writing, 45
Business location, 88–99

Cash forecast, 63
Commitments, family, 9, 12
Computers, 130–132
Consultants, 141
CoSIRA, 25, 69, 157
Costings, 125–130
Customers, 125

Department of Employment, 57, 157
Department of Trade and Industry, 69, 157
Direct Selling Association, 55, 159
Dismissal, 138

Enterprise Allowance Scheme, 68–69
Employers' liability, 144
Employment, contracts, 135–136
Estate agents, 140–141
Expenses,
   allowable, 78
   capital, 78
Experience, commercial, 26

Family credit, 81
Finance,
  assessing, 58–59
  personal, 11–14
  sources of, 66–70
Franchising, 108–110

Government Guaranteed Loan Scheme, 67
Grants, student, 82

Insurance, 92, 96, 141–143
Insurance, brokers, 140
Insurance, National (see under National Insurance)
Interviewing, 134–135
Investors in Industry, 69
Issued capital, 106

Job Centre, 27

Labour,
  direct, 60
  indirect, 60
Limited companies, 105–107
Liquidation, 152–153
Loss of profits, 143–144

Manpower Services Commission, 27
Marketing, 117
Memorandum of Association, 106

National Farmers' Union, 55, 159
National Insurance, 65, 79, 126, 137–138

Partnerships, 71, 102–105
PAYE (see under tax)
Pensions, 81
Professional indemnity, 144
Profit plan, 59–61
Property,
  buying, 98–99
  freehold, 98, 99
  leasing, 94–97
  renting, 95
Public relations, 120–122

Receivership, 150
Recruitment, 133–134
Redundancy, 139
Redundancy payments, 81

Research,
  product, 25
  market, 32–34
Retraining, 28–29

Selling, 111–117
Skills, personal, 21, 22
Sole trading, 100–102
Solicitors, 139–140
Statutory sick pay, 83, 147
Statutory maternity pay, 82, 137
Stock, 128–129
Suppliers, 126, 132

Tax,
  and the self-employed, 77
  Capital Gains, 86, 92, 99
  Corporation, 84
  Inheritance, 87
  PAYE, 65, 137–138, 153
  VAT, 64, 84, 127, 152, 153
Time management, 20
Tourism, 70
Tourist boards, 70, 158
Training,
  formal, 27
  full-time, 27–28
  informal, 29
  part-time, 27